CHOOSING TO READ

Connecting Middle Schoolers to Books

CHOOSING TO READ

with essays from

san campbell bartoletti

michael buckley

jack gantos

jeff kinney

gordon korman

jon scieszka

paul volponi

jacqueline woodson

Heinemann
361 Hanover Street
Portsmouth, NH 03801–3912
www.heinemann.com

Offices and agents throughout the world

The author and publisher wish to thank those who have generously given permission to reprint borrowed material:

Susan Campbell Bartoletti's essay copyright © 2012 by Susan Campbell Bartoletti. Used by permission of the author.

"He ate and drank the precious words" from *The Poems of Emily Dickinson*, Thomas H. Johnson, Editor, Cambridge, MA: The Belknap Press of Harvard University Press. Copyright © 1951, 1955, 1979, 1983 by the President and Fellows of Harvard College.

Chapter 1 and Appendix D adapted from "If You Want Students to Read—Motivate Them" by Joan Kindig in *Exemplary Instruction in the Middle Grades: Teaching That Supports Engagement and Rigorous Learning* edited by Diane Lapp and Barbara Moss. Copyright © 2012 by the Guilford Press. Used by permission of the publisher.

Excerpt from blog entry "Student-led Book Clubs" by Sarah Mulhern, posted June 13, 2009 on The Reading Zone: http://thereadingzone.wordpress.com/2009/06/13/student-led-book-clubs/. Used by permission of the author.

"Quick Picks for Reluctant Young Adult Readers—Selection Criteria" by the Young Adult Library Services Association, a division of the American Library Association: http://www.ala.org/yalsa/booklistsawards/booklists/quickpicks/quickpicksreluctantyoung. Used by permission of the publisher.

Library of Congress Cataloging-in-Publication Data
Kindig, Joan Schroeder.
    Choosing to read : connecting middle schoolers to books / Joan Schroeder Kindig ; foreword by Laura Robb.
        pages   cm
    Includes bibliographical references.
    ISBN-13: 978-0-325-03144-6
    ISBN-10: 0-325-03144-4
    1. Middle school students—Books and reading—United States.   2. Reading (Middle school)—United States.   3. Reading—Remedial teaching—United States.   4. Reading promotion—United States.   5. Young adult literature—Bibliography.   6. High interest-low vocabulary books—Bibliography.   I. Title.
    Z1037.A1K5319   2012
    025.5'5—dc23   2012017309

Acquiring editor: Margaret LaRaia
Editor: Tobey Antao
Developmental editor: Alan Huisman
Production: Victoria Merecki
Typesetter: Cape Cod Compositors, Inc.
Cover and interior designs: Lisa Fowler
Cover photos: Top photo © Sean De Burca/Getty Images. Bottom photo © Dominic DiSaia/Getty Images.
Manufacturing: Steve Bernier

Printed in the United States of America on acid-free paper

16   15   14   13   12   VP   1   2   3   4   5

Dedication

To the two smartest and kindest men I know, both of whom had the
most profound impact on my life: Harold J. Schroeder Jr., my father,
who would have been so proud to see my name on this book, and
to my son, Nick Kindig, whom I am proud of every day.

Also to Laura Robb, teacher extraordinaire, who is both my fairy
godmother and my biggest cheerleader.

Contents

Foreword

Choosing to Read: Connecting Middle Schoolers to Books by Joan Kindig is an important book—a seminal book—for teachers and librarians. I read *Choosing to Read* in two sittings because I felt compelled to read, read, read. Joan's voice is powerful, engaging, and humorous, and I connected deeply to her literacy stories about middle school students, teachers, and parents.

I sighed, holding the manuscript to my chest, when I came to the extensive bibliography that marked the end of the text. I did not want this book to end, and I continually find myself rereading parts, replaying and skimming favorite literacy stories, conversational reflections by young adult authors, and annotated book lists. I've raided my public library, checking out and reading book recommendations that I haven't read, and I find that I have a wealth of books to recommend to students and teachers as well as titles I believe every school library should have. Joan has transformed my reading life just as I know she will transform yours!

This is an important book for experienced teachers and those new to the profession. Joan's extensive knowledge of adolescent literature is a guiding beacon for teachers who seek to motivate and engage their students by helping them develop literary tastes and a rich, personal reading life! In addition, Joan emphasizes that choice—students choosing books they want to read, on topics they care about and topics that interest them—creates lifelong readers.

This is an important book for new teachers, who will celebrate Joan's authentic suggestions for independent and instructional reading—suggestions that encourage deep and meaningful discussions of themes, ideas, characters, and information. All teachers will revel in the extensive, annotated book lists for middle school students who are developing readers in need of middle school books they can read and comprehend, or titles that appeal to skilled and proficient readers. You'll return to those rich book lists again and again—lists such as 100 picture books for older readers, the nine page bibliography of children's books cited, and the featured book lists in every chapter.

This is an important book for librarians, teachers, and students because Joan includes short and memorable reflections on reading by some of the best, most beloved, and widely read young adult authors. Reading pieces by Jacqueline Woodson, Jack Gantos, Gordon Korman, Jeff Kinney, Susan Campbell Bartoletti, Jon Scieszka, Michael Buckley, and Paul Volponi will resonate with and inspire students who can see and connect to aspects of their reading lives in the stories the authors share. In Appendix E, Joan has included a list of works by the contributing authors—another invaluable resource.

This is an important book because Joan Kindig annually reads and evaluates all the newly published books for middle school students. She has gathered up her knowledge of and experience with using young adult books with teachers and students and has stamped every page of *Choosing to Read: Connecting Middle Schoolers to Books* with her passion for reading.

Emily Dickinson captures the essence and importance of this book when she explains that a book is a "bequest of wings" because books, reading, nurture the soul and enlarge the spirit.

> *He ate and drank the precious words;*
> *His spirit grew robust;*
> *He knew no more that he was poor,*
> *Nor that his frame was dust.*
> *He danced along the dingy days,*
> *And this bequest of wings*
> *Was but a book—what liberty*
> *A loosened spirit brings!*

—*Laura Robb*

Acknowledgments

An author is indeed lucky to find one great editor whose work style approximates her own—one who makes the process so much less daunting and offers suggestions that make all the difference in the completed manuscript. Lucky me, I found two! Thanks to Margaret LaRaia who started me out, helped me find my voice, and saw me well on my way until her maternity leave intervened. Margaret paired me with Tobey Antao who picked up without missing a beat, kept me focused, and who saw this project expertly through to the end. I couldn't have found better or kinder editors to work with than these two women.

Thanks to my colleague at James Madison University, Gay Ivey, whose work in adolescent literacy has informed so many of us. Our many conversations about middle schoolers and reading made me even more excited about this project.

While I started this book before I was invited in to Warren County Middle School to work with the teachers in changing their reading program, this book would not be as rich without that wonderful opportunity. Thanks to the principal, Alan Fox, whose leadership allows his teachers to become the best they can be. The teachers were the best, and to each of them a heartfelt thank you. To Cathi Ballard, Amanda Burton, Anne Merrin Clemmer, Jamie Dusing, Tim Gunn, Jessica Hendrickson, Kara Kocon, Danelle Sperling, and Rebecca Webster, many thanks for letting me into your classrooms.

Special thanks to my graduate assistant, Ashleigh Shepherd, who helped with compiling all the surveys and procuring articles for me. She saved me endless time, and it was truly appreciated.

Finally, a huge thank-you goes to Laura Robb, for whom I have the deepest respect as a person and as an educator. It was Laura who suggested I share my ideas in a book, and here we are. Her work with children and teachers over her long career gives me much to aspire to.

*A*n Invitation to Change

Teachers are some of the bravest people I know. We go into classrooms every day to face kids, some who are eager to read and learn, some who tolerate school but can be motivated if we work hard enough, some who adamantly refuse to participate in their own learning. Because we are expected to teach every child, our task increases exponentially. The kids who are eager to read and learn are a piece of cake. The ones who have to be jumpstarted are at least capable of being reached. But what about those who see reading and school as something to be endured, who seem to be daring you to teach them? It's no surprise that we worry about these kids. But we worry about those who are not particularly keen as well.

Some of the kids in our classrooms are not reading. How can that be? We choose strong literature that has stood the test of time and assign it as part of our language arts or English class. It should be a slam-dunk. But the truth is, kids don't read their assignments (for a variety of reasons, which I discuss in this book). If what we are doing is not working as well as we'd hoped, shouldn't we consider a change that could make all the difference in the world to the students in our classes?

What is it we ultimately want for our students? We want them to have options that will allow them to fit into this world in whatever way they desire. To do anything well, they have to be decent readers. But more than just becoming decent readers, we want them to *want* to read. Our country is built on the notion of an educated, voting populace, and being able to read and use the knowledge we gain from reading is essential. Through reading, learning becomes something students own, something that can sustain them throughout their lives.

I ask you to consider an approach to teaching reading that is different from the one you are used to. If what you are doing is not working for many of your kids, what have you got to lose?

There is always some risk when trying something new, and risk and change can be scary. In this book I walk you through what it will take to change your reading program from one that isn't getting the results you want to one that allows for student choice, entices children with books that are relevant to their lives, and turns kids into real readers.

Teachers are brave. And anyway, scary doesn't matter as long as the students make progress—any good teacher will tell you that. Are you ready to dip your toes in the water?

Setting the Stage

MAKING A CASE FOR CHOICE

Teachers are the most well-meaning people in the world. When we find a book that we think kids should read, we don't give up until the child walks away with that book tucked under his or her arm. Pressing a book we think is important on a student can't cause any harm, can it? I heard Michael Buckley tell this story about being a reluctant reader and I immediately asked him to write it up for this book. Behind the funny story he tells is a bit of pathos, though. As a kid, he wasn't much of a reader and ended up shying away from reading because all the books grown-ups thought he *should* read bored him to tears. He assumed all books were boring based on what he had been forced to read. It was only when an adult gave him a book that she thought *he* would like that he found a book that captivated him. In this chapter I will be talking about choice and how important that is for kids. If Michael had been allowed to choose his own books rather than being told to read books his teachers thought he should read, he might have become an engaged reader sooner than the ripe old age of nine!

Jacqueline Woodson's piece tells of her daughter, Toshi, and the kinds of reading she's enjoying most right now at age nine. Toshi is well acquainted with good books from the family read-alouds and the books that are all over the house. What is she choosing to read though? Not what "we the teacher" or "we the parent" might want. Still, Toshi is reading and is enjoying some new formats and some old ones as well. Toshi is a reader, and as long as she is reading she's going to be just fine. After all, I read my favorite comic series, Herbie Popnecker (totally excellent), again and again at about her age. I remember those comics vividly. Some are still in my closet. Having the choice to read those books let me spread my wings and made me love reading even more. I think Toshi will be like me. I remained engaged in print (a comic book *is* reading!) and am a lifelong reader. It is true—there is life after comic books.

When I was nine years old I was a pain in the ass. These days the proper term is "reluctant reader," but back then "pain in the ass" got the job done. I was one of those kids that hated reading. I avoided books and steered clear of the library, which was widely known by most boys in the fourth grade as the place where a good day went to die.

I wasn't being difficult on purpose. I might have been an avid reader if not for the good intentions of well-meaning teachers. They frequently pressed books into my hands, but they weren't books they thought I'd like. They were books they thought I *should* like; girls living on the prairie, boys with deer for pets, children who have to shoot a beloved family dog, etc.... Growing up in a bustling city I couldn't relate to the characters or their old-fashioned experiences. Their messages about being a good person had all the subtlety of a mallet to the head, too. They bored me.

Luckily, our school librarian noticed. She cornered me in the hallway, and with an extended finger she said, "Mr. Buckley, follow me."

Any pain in the ass knows that when an adult combines a formal title with your last name you're in for some kind of trouble, but I was smart enough to do as I was told. Together the librarian and I marched through a labyrinth of shelves packed tight with books. Eventually she found the one she wanted and shoved it into my hand, demanding I tell her everything about it in two weeks.

It was called *The Mouse and the Motorcycle*.

I begrudgingly opened it that night, certain the mouse would be rabid by page 30 and soon come face-to-face with a frontier kid's shotgun. I was convinced I would hate it because I hated every book adults gave me. I was wrong. I loved it! Mainly because it had the three most important elements that a reluctant reader wants in a book:

1. It's a big adventure.
2. It's funny.
3. It's completely pointless.

There is no heavy-handed moral lesson in *The Mouse and the Motorcycle*. I wasn't supposed to learn anything from it. It didn't ask me to be a better person. It was just fun and it showed me that reading could be entertaining rather than a sermon about good morals. It transformed me from a pain into a reader, and when I returned to the library I was eager for more. Cleary's classic is still my favorite book of all time, and I might not have discovered it if the librarian had kept thinking about what I should like rather than what I would like. Eventually, I read all the things I was supposed to like. Some of them I actually did, but it all started because someone gave me a book she knew I would love.

FEATURED AUTHOR: Jacqueline Woodson

I am watching my nine-year-old daughter become a reluctant reader and it's making me crazy. She sits and reads for hours and has to be told to put her reading away at dinnertime. She has read Raina Telgemeier's *Smile* nine times (and plans to read it for the tenth time when she turns ten in a year). She's gone through *The Baby Sitter's Club* that Raina illustrated (not the straight-up text ones!). She can give you the lowdown on every character in the cast of Archie, laughs out loud at Calvin and Hobbes, sneaks pages of picture books, long after Lights Out.

When the family read *The Watsons Go to Birmingham* together out loud, she was mad when the book ended, wondering why Christopher Paul Curtis didn't just keep on writing. Same with our family read of *Bud Not Buddy*.

Still, in third grade, my child's favorite way to pass the time is to sit curled around a comic book. "Mommy," she admitted to me one afternoon as we walked home from the school bus. "You understand why I'm not a fan of your work, right?"

"Actually, Toshi. I don't."

"Well, it's just *not funny*."

Comic books are funny. And left to her own devices, she'd never put them down. In the same way, my brothers, her uncles Hope and Roman, read comics nonstop as young boys.

But in the public school system—now, as it was so back then—comics are not considered a part of reading. No matter that many have a narrative arc, character development, words that are sometimes new and unfamiliar. Hence, my daughter is a reluctant reader. She likes pictures. She likes comedy. She loves characters with snappy answers and good fashion.

Her teacher is encouraging though—offering her book after book, hoping to keep the energy going while moving her nose (at least a little bit) out of the pages of comics. I'm torn. I want her to read the books I loved as a kid. I want the pictures to disappear from the narratives. I want Archie gone from my house! But I am the one who gave her her first Archie comic book. I am the one who laughs at slapstick with her. I am the one who gets the silly jokes and sneak-reads her comics when sleep gets the best of her and they drop from her hand. And I am the child-now-grown who read *Mad* magazine and picture books and Sunday comics until I thought I'd pass out from laughter. And she is my child. So here we are. Go figure.

TURNING TURNED-OFF READERS ON TO CHOICE

*I*n curricular debates there are always those who argue vehemently for teaching the same books taught to us as children: the literary canon. They've been taught for ages, so why change now? These are classics, aren't they? Don't we want our kids reading the classics? Embedded in the argument for the literary canon is a philosophy of teaching that places the book above the needs of the student reading it. On Dictionary.com, *canon* is defined as "any officially recognized set of sacred books." The word *sacred* here means *unassailable, inviolable*. And word choices, as any good reader or literary critic will tell you, are important. The word *classic* suggests more than a mere book.

Words like that make me ask why. Why should a book be elevated to the status of necessary and inviolable? What makes it so distinctive that all kids must read it? First, I take issue with the concept of a "canon." Many kids define themselves as nonreaders because of their lack of success with these books. It's the I-can't-read-that-book-so-I'm-not-a-reader syndrome. The needs of our students should come before the need to read any one book. It is more important to find something the kids can and will read than require a book that is beyond their reading skill and irrelevant to them. Second, we don't *teach* books, we expose children to books and all the beauty and wonder they contain—the rhythm of the language, the turns of phrase, the perfect word choices, the descriptions of the setting, the facets of the characters, the theme—I could go on and on.

A TALE OF *A TALE OF TWO CITIES*

Twenty middle schoolers pour through the classroom doorway. There's lots of chatter—these social creatures are busy catching up on everything from Taylor Swift's recent concert to the latest movie they saw—until the bell rings and they dutifully take their seats. On every desk is a copy of *A Tale of Two Cities*.

"What's this?" they want to know, eyeing the book suspiciously.

"I'm glad you're interested," their teacher says, and begins discussing the importance of the one-size-fits-all book she expects even the weakest readers to read. The kids hear *Dickens, the late 1700s, French Revolution*, and *classic*. Silence falls. Here, once again, is a book they have no connection with and no interest in; many of them also have no possibility of being able to read it. Read this excerpt and think about all the hurdles a middle school student might encounter when trying to (a) decode it, (b) understand it, and (c) be interested in it:

> *If you could say, with truth, to your own solitary heart, to-night, 'I have secured to myself the love and attachment, the gratitude or respect, of no human creature; I have won myself a tender place in no regard; I have done nothing good or serviceable to be remembered by!' your seventy-eight years would be seventy-eight heavy curses; would they not?*

I have trouble really getting it myself!

The hurdles include:

- *Textual difficulties.* Archaic language is off-putting to today's teen readers—it's difficult to understand—and topics in the classics tend to be arcane and don't particularly resonate. The diction and punctuation in *A Tale of Two Cities* place the book stylistically in the Victorian period. Unless you have an unusual kid in your class (and maybe you do), this way of speaking will be unfamiliar, and trying to understand every sentence will be a chore. Would you willingly read a book that required that much effort?

- *Required background knowledge.* *A Tale of Two Cities* was written by a Victorian author (over 150 years ago) about the French Revolution (approximately 220 years ago), so an understanding of both time periods is helpful to understanding the book. Those are quite a few hoops for developing readers to jump through. Do you think they will?

- *Lack of relevance.* Although the messages of *A Tale of Two Cities* can be related to a middle schooler's life (the desire to be known for something other than our worst mistakes, for example), a lot of work is required for the typical student to make this connection. How many of your kids are motivated enough or skilled enough at making inferences to do this?

Look with fresh eyes at the books you have given students over the years. Would any of your students have encountered the problems above? A book with even one of these problems is likely one that most kids faked their way through. That is, they read the SparkNotes or simply tuned out completely. Outward compliance doesn't mean students are doing what you ask them to do. They can be pretty resourceful when avoiding tasks they know they are not good at. I did it when I was a teenager.

Now, I'm not kicking off an anti-Dickens campaign. I don't mean for one minute that Dickens did not produce some incredible books. Some, like *A Christmas Carol*, are defining elements of our culture. In a perfect world all middle school kids (well, eighth graders anyway) would be able to read his work, and my great hope is that one day they will be able to pick up *Oliver Twist* and see it for the great social commentary it is, a snapshot of the Victorian era, warts and all. It's this desire that drives a great many teachers to give students these classic but archaic books.

I believe strongly, as they do, that reading is the ability to access information and that our democracy depends on a population that can read critically. We part ways on the classics, though. I feel teachers must consider where students are as readers, both their reading level and what they are interested in reading, before we give any book to them to read. The reality of schools today is that there are no homogenous classes in which all kids are reading on grade level. There are also no classes in which all the kids are eager to read; some readers have to be shown that books are accessible if chosen carefully and if what is in them is worth reading. We have to put our lofty ideals aside and trust that if we get kids reading and show them what awaits them in the world of books, they will one day find Dickens and enjoy and appreciate him.

Cut to a very different classroom in which seventh graders have their noses deep in their books, are passionate about what they're doing. I walk around looking at the titles, asking kids what they're reading and what they think about what they're reading. One series that keeps popping up is The Chronicles of Vladimir Tod, by Heather Brewer. I have seen the books—you can't miss the distinctive logo, a happy face with vampire fangs—but haven't read them yet. I read the first book in the series, *Eighth Grade Bites*, the next day and see immediately what draws young readers to it. Vlad Tod, who has a human mother and a vampire father, has all the problems a middle schooler has fitting in, but a few more of the vampire variety as well. Vampire stories are popular right now, but looking beyond the vampire aspect, this is a story about a kid their own age with the same problems they have. It's a perfect fit, not hard to sell.

Dickens is great, but wouldn't Heather Brewer's series be more likely to pull middle schoolers into the world of books instead of pushing them away? They're an opening through which to pull students even further into the world of books. They've had a positive reading experience and now know what we all know: there are some great books out there. "If you liked that one, you might like this one" is on the tip of our tongue.

Weak, unpracticed readers aren't that way because they haven't applied themselves. When I was a child, I was miserable at math. My father, a chemical engineer, used math every day and was darn good at it. When I was (often) frustrated by my math homework, Dad would offer to help me. No matter what he tried, I just couldn't get it. He would say that it was easy if I would only apply myself. What he didn't realize, and what many teachers don't realize about reading, is that I wanted to get the math as much as he wanted me to get it. Being rotten at math wasn't about not applying myself; it was about being outside my abilities and my comfort zone. I could work twenty-four/seven and still not get it—it was conceptually beyond me. It's the same with our struggling readers who somehow didn't get it in their early school years and now are expected to read a difficult text like *A Tale of Two Cities* when it is well beyond their abilities at that moment in time no matter how hard they apply themselves.

TRY IT OUT
Reflect on Your Reading Life

Think about yourself as a reader, both when you were young and now as an adult. Take a few minutes and write down your answers to these questions:

- Did you have difficulty learning to read? What did that feel like?
- What kinds of things did you read as child?
- Were you an avid reader or one who read only when forced? How about comic books or magazines?
- Did you ever resort to CliffNotes or SparkNotes instead of reading an assigned book?

- Where do you stand as an adult reader? Does your hectic teaching schedule and family life preclude reading, or is lying in bed at night with a good book a bedtime ritual?
- What was the last adult book you read?
- What was the last children's or young adult book you read and why did you read it?
- How does thinking about these questions help put what kids choose to read into perspective?

REFORMING MIDDLE SCHOOL READING INSTRUCTION

I have spent the last year working with the teachers at Warren County Middle School (WCMS), a rural middle school (sixth and seventh grades) in Virginia. There had been a growing concern among teachers and administrators that the students were not making real progress in reading. They had a good pass rate on the state tests but were not readers in the real sense of the word.

This is not an isolated concern. The 2005 National Assessment of Education Progress (NAEP) showed that students' intrinsic motivation—their desire to read—had declined over the three-year period 2002–2005. A nationally representative survey of fourth graders that same year (Donahue et al. 2005) revealed that fourth graders' attitudes toward reading were bleak. Only 35 percent listed reading as a favorite activity. How sad that two-thirds of fourth graders did not read books regularly and eagerly! To make matters worse, 73 percent reported that they did not read frequently for enjoyment, and 59 percent said they didn't learn much when they read.

Rebecca Webster, one of the sixth-grade language arts teachers at the Virginia school, felt her very traditional program was not serving her students. The kids weren't reading what she assigned in class and weren't talking about anything they were reading at home either. She read *The Book Whisperer: Awakening the Inner Reader in Every Child*, by Donalyn Miller (2009), and thought these ideas might be a way to jumpstart her students. Her enthusiasm got some of the other teachers interested too, and before long they got their principal on board as well. Although the approach was new to them, it has been used successfully in many classrooms since Nancie Atwell first published *In the Middle* (1987). With the support of their language arts coordinator, their principal, and a literacy grant, the teachers put the anthologies aside (but still within reach), along with the one-size-fits-all approach, and began using authentic texts in their classroom.

This is where I came in. I am a professor of reading whose specialty is children's and young adult (YA) literature. I know how kids come to reading, what will keep them reading, and the YA and children's book market. I read the same books these kids do, so I am a good resource for teachers wishing to move from anthologies to real books.

In the fall of 2009 I gave a survey (see Appendix A) to these sixth and seventh graders. I needed to know where they were as readers and how they felt about reading in general. Six hundred twenty-six kids turned in a survey, and the results were more encouraging than the NAEP numbers above. Thirty-nine percent said they loved to read, 44 percent said they read only when they had to, and 17 percent reported that they hated to read.

Although I am comparing apples and oranges to some extent, in both my and Donahue's survey, only a little more than a third of the kids reported that they loved to read or that reading was a favorite activity. I would have loved that number to be higher, but given that the media report every day that kids aren't reading and schools are failing, I felt that 35–39 percent of readers was a fairly strong base. And while only 27 percent of the respondents in Donahue's survey said they read for enjoyment, 56 percent of my middle schoolers (double!) read when they didn't have to. I was thrilled. Over half of my kids liked to read, even though for some of them it wasn't their favorite thing to do. These were kids I could prompt to read more and more by engaging them. And I was heartened to know that only 17 percent of the kids hated to read. That's still almost a fifth of the population, but most of the kids had a decent attitude toward reading and that would make my job easier.

I came up with a lengthy list of books for the school to purchase with the literacy grant, and we jumped in: we gave real kids real books to read.

Not Just Books: Expanding Our Concept of Reading

My opening icebreaker in every class I teach preservice teachers at James Madison University is some version of the earlier reflecting-on-your-reading-life activity. The students tell me they are so busy that pleasure reading has fallen by the wayside; however, I find out that they read poetry, nonfiction, contemporary realistic fiction, lots of fantasy, bestsellers, some self-help, mysteries, magazines, and more recently, graphic novels. Gender differences arise, but to my surprise Stephenie Meyer's Twilight series appears in both camps. This starts a grand conversation about why we read—for the beauty of the language, to learn, to see ourselves vicariously in another's situation, to entertain, and to escape.

When I began this exercise, I had to expand my definition of reading. I am embarrassed to admit that I thought romance novels weren't "reading" and that magazine readers weren't "real" readers either. Reading is reading, and everything we or a child picks up has something worthwhile to offer. A romance novel has a setting, characters, a problem that needs resolution, and all the other story elements we teach. I am not suggesting that we bring romance novels into fifth-grade classrooms, but I am suggesting that we open up the definition of what reading is to better serve our children. Graphic novels are a great way to get kids reading, and there are terrific ones out there. I know you can think of at least one or two children in your classroom who would read a NASCAR magazine far more readily than a novel. Both Piaget and Vygotsky encourage us to begin where the child is. If a magazine will lure a child to the written page, I'm all for it—and for a fairly sneaky reason. I know that once I get children reading, I have a much better chance of nudging them toward something more worthwhile. If they are not reading, it's nearly impossible.

The Elephant in the Room: They're Not Reading What We Assign!

My college students read all kinds of things as children. Many of them can recall favorite picture books like *Miss Nelson Is Missing* (Allard 1977), *Goodnight Moon* (Brown 1947), or *The True Story of the 3 Little Pigs!* (Scieszka 1989) and often revisit them during my children's literature class. *If* and *what* you read as a child impacts whether you read as an adult. What is most interesting is the diversity of choices my students made as young readers. They had genre preferences, sometimes wanted a short book versus a long book (don't we all at some point!), their interests were reflected in what they read, and typical gender preferences were obvious. Most had not read the "classics" until they reached middle school when assigned reading reared its ugly head. They went from self-selecting (within parameters) to being forced to read things that reflected none of their previous preferences. The majority of them report that their reading fell off during middle and high school, a characteristic well documented in the research. I ask them to raise their hand if they ever re-sorted to SparkNotes, and nearly every student in every class does. These are the students who made it to college! Their reading fell off because of the many hurdles that had to be negotiated when reading books they were not interested in.

READER PROFILE ▶ Assigned Reading Often Isn't Read

Porter, a high school senior, quickly decides he isn't going to read *Beowulf*, the class assignment. Instead, he listens intently to class discussions, takes the test, and scores 80 out of 100. (He didn't even bother to buy the SparkNotes.) His teacher knows he didn't read the book, but she feels she has no choice but to give him a B because he answered enough questions correctly to merit that grade. What is accomplished by this exercise? No reading has been done, there is no appreciation for the work itself, and Porter has improved his avoidance skills. Not exactly what the well-meaning teacher had in mind, is it? In effect, she gave Porter choices when she required him to read *Beowulf*. Read the book, struggle through it and feel dumb, or circumvent her by getting the SparkNotes, or just wing it. It speaks to the inappropriateness of *Beowulf* in high school that Porter didn't even attempt to read it. He didn't see the relevance of this monster story to his life, and the archaic language only confirmed it. If we acknowledge his choice *not* to read what he was assigned, we recognize that allowing kids to choose what they read is an effective and powerful tool. Let's give them positive choices—choices of what to read, not rea-sons to avoid reading. Kids will read better and discuss their reading better as they read more and more books they care about. When I asked Porter what he learned from this he said, "You gotta be engaged in what you're reading or else," identifying something that most people fail to recognize. Engagement and relevance are key.

Guiding Principles for Identifying Books Kids Will Read

The hurdles presented by the literary canon can become guiding principles to help us match kids with the right books and, more important, help kids realize that the problem isn't that they're not a reader but that they're not reading the right book.

- We need to be aware of the *difficulty* of any text we put on our shelves. Middle school teachers probably have students with reading levels rang-ing from second grade through high school. We need books for each of the reading levels represented in our classroom so that all kids get to par-ticipate fully in what goes on there. A one-size-fits-all approach to read-ing keeps weak readers weak. A reader at the second-grade level might enjoy the Time Warp Trio series, by Jon Scieszka (Viking). The books are funny and don't look like they're for really young children (humor is sophisticated, and kids love it). A reader at the fourth-grade level might find the Bone graphic novel series engaging. Readers at the sixth-grade level and above might love the Harry Potter series or any of the books by Gordon Korman. *The Chronicles of Vladimir Tod: Eighth Grade Bites* (Brewer 2007) will be a hit as well. And how about *Locomotion* (2003) and *Peace, Locomotion* (2009), by Jacqueline Woodson, for kids reading at the fourth-through eighth-grade level?

- *Background knowledge* should always be front and center when choosing books for students. Forcing kids into texts dealing with topics or situations about which they know nothing means they will get little from what they are reading. Kids who lack the necessary background knowledge need additional support. This can take many forms: brainstorming, reading another text aloud that fills them in, or sharing a relevant story. For example, I introduced a fantastic book called *Phineas Gage: A Gruesome but True Story of Brain Science* (Fleischman 2002) to seventh and eighth graders by telling them about a teen I knew who suffered frontal lobe damage in a drunk-driving accident. After I had described the effect the accident had on the girl's personality and her emotional range, the kids *ran* to sign out the book, their interest was so piqued.

- *Relevance* may very well be the most important of these three components of engagement. If students find a book's content interesting, getting them to read it is a piece of cake. We live in a fascinating age with information everywhere. Why not tap into what interests kids? Relevance motivates reluctant readers more than anything else. When the first book in the Harry Potter series came out, kids everywhere were reading it. Many children who were not up to the challenges it presented read it anyway because they wanted to be part of the phenomenon. Reading above one's instructional reading level does not as a rule improve reading prowess. But once in a while, with books as great as the Harry Potters, no problem! *Treasure Island*, by Robert Louis Stevenson, and *The Red Badge of Courage* by Stephen Crane, are not relevant to students today, and kids will not push themselves to get through them. Although these books are often referred to as timeless tales, they are incredibly dated. If our aim is to engage kids, we need to look to books that reflect the world kids today live in, like *Pop*, by Gordon Korman (2009); *If I Stay*, by Gayle Forman (2009); and *The Lightning Thief*, by Rick Riordan (2005).

Read any two of the following outstanding books for middle schoolers. You will have a new perspective on how well written these books are and why teens are so interested in them.

1. *Speak*, by Laurie Halse Anderson (1999: contemporary realistic fiction, Printz Honor Book). Melinda starts freshman year as an outcast after she calls the police to a preschool party. She is ostracized and never talks to anyone at school. Everyone—including the reader—thinks she called the cops because of a holier-than-thou attitude toward underage drinking. During the course of the year, the reader learns what happened to Melinda that night and how she begins to find her voice once again. This story features a strong but vulnerable female protagonist who copes as best she can after a rape. A great book for both teen boys and girls.

2. *If I Stay*, by Gayle Forman (2009: contemporary realistic fiction). On a snowy day, Mia and her family go out for a drive to see the beautiful scenery near their home. There is an accident, and only Mia and her younger brother Teddy survive. The story is told from Mia's point of view as she lies in a coma trying to understand what has happened to her family. She learns that her parents were killed and that, after a touch-and-go day, Teddy dies as well. Her loss is so intense that she feels like giving up. They say that surviving a traumatic event like this takes a will to live, and Mia doesn't seem to have it. She has to make a choice: Do I stay or don't I?

3. *Tangerine*, by Edward Bloor (1997: contemporary realistic fiction). Paul's older brother Erik is the town's golden boy. He's a great football player, and the family's life revolves around Erik's going to college to play ball and eventually go pro. Paul is less athletic, is visually impaired, and feels inferior compared with his brother. But Paul sees a side of Erik that no one else sees and realizes that the hero is severely flawed. What happens to Erik when he goes a step too far? The twist at the end of this story is amazing.

4. *A Northern Light*, by Jennifer Donnelly (2003: historical fiction, Printz Honor Book). This literary novel based on Theodore Dreiser's *An American Tragedy* reexplores the reality that who you are and who your family is might impact the measure of justice you receive. It is beautifully written and a worthy update of a classic.

5. *Monster*, by Walter Dean Myers (1999: contemporary realistic fiction, Printz Award). Steven is an African American teen from a caring, involved family who wants what is best for their son. He is on the right track in school until he meets up with some punks from the neighborhood and accompanies them to what turns out to be a holdup. The reader is never sure about the level of Steven's complicity, but he was outside when the shots rang out and the grocery clerk fell dead. Is Steven responsible for the clerk's death? Has he aided and abetted? Would he be facing charges if he were a white kid? This is an incredible story of responsibility and culpability that really gets teens talking.

6. *Thirteen Reasons Why*, by Jay Asher (2007: contemporary realistic fiction). Clay receives a package that contains cassette tapes made by his friend Hannah, who recently committed suicide. She made the tapes to let the thirteen people who contributed to her wanting to end her life know what they did to her. Teen readers take away the reality that the petty things they do to joke with or hurt their classmates can have a profound effect. Bullying is highlighted in a wonderful and insightful way.

7. *The Future of Us*, by Jay Asher and Carolyn Mackler (2011: fantasy). The year is 1996, before the Internet was as powerful as it is today. Emma receives a computer from her dad, installs the accompanying AOL CD, and begins surfing. She logs into a site called Facebook and looks up herself and some of her friends. What she finds is shocking—she's married, she didn't do all the things she hoped to do beforehand, and her life is completely different from what she hoped. The reader knows Facebook didn't appear online until 2004. What is going on? If Emma, and later, her friend Josh, can see the future, will what they do today influence what happens tomorrow? This is a terrific novel about choices and where they lead us.

8. *The Absolutely True Diary of a Part-Time Indian*, by Sherman Alexie (2007: contemporary realistic fiction/multicultural). Junior is a kid on the reservation who is able to see beyond the fences that surround his people. He is tired of the way Native Americans are treated and the rampant alcoholism, and wants to find a better path for himself. He decides to leave the reservation to attend the local school, and life there turns out to have its own problems. This somewhat autobiographical novel is part hilarity and part pathos, but it paints a very accurate picture of life as Native Americans see it.

9. *The Hunger Games*, by Suzanne Collins (2008: fantasy). In this futuristic novel, Katniss has been selected to represent her district at the Hunger Games. The teens chosen for this reality-type television show must fight to the death in order to survive. Alliances are formed as these embattled kids play out the contest, a twisted way for the government to control its citizens. This is a great look at what is done in the name of patriotism and government control. The other books in the Hunger Games trilogy are *Catching Fire* and *Mockingjay*.

10. *Feed*, by M. T. Anderson (2002: fantasy). The book is set in a future in which all of us have an implant in our brain that feeds us information—all about the jeans being advertised on the billboard we're passing, for example. The feed is beginning to run our lives. When the feed malfunctions one day, everything changes. Can we think for ourselves? Do we even want to anymore?

Choice Means a Greater Likelihood of Meeting State Standards

If you ask teachers what books state standards dictate they cover, they come up with a short list of classics, occasionally throwing in *To Kill a Mockingbird*, by Harper Lee (1960), or *The Outsiders*, by S. E. Hinton (1967), to make their lists appear up to date. While both books are extraordinary and I count them among my favorites, there are SparkNotes for them because teachers use them so much. Mightn't more recent titles be added to the list as well?

Our job as teachers is to make sure kids can read, and to do that we have to get them reading. The way to do *that* is to offer them relevant books that they can read. After we have them engaged, we can talk about the elements of story and the wonderful techniques authors sometimes use like foreshadowing and point of view. We can discuss books based on their themes and ask kids to support their opinions about what the author was trying to achieve. In short, we can meet all the standards set by our school curriculum and state standards in books that are being published today.

After spending a day with my "adopted" middle schoolers at WCMS, I spent time with the faculty. One of their questions was, "How can we cover the state standards and still offer the kids choice?" I pulled out the Virginia Standards of Learning for sixth and seventh grades (which are not unique: every state's standards tend to be similar) and went over them one by one. Not only would every standard be covered, it would be covered in spades. In addition, the standards helped us brainstorm a list of possible topics for mini-lessons during the coming year. Increased interaction with print brings all kinds of positive results.

Furthermore, the Virginia state standards don't mention by name any of the "classic" texts that teachers have been assigning year after year. Nor are they are mentioned in the NCTE/IRA standards. Titles are suggested in the Common Core State Standards (CCSS)—unfortunately, with an average publishing date of 1930 and a most recent one of 1976—but they are not mandated. While 1976 might not feel all that long ago to most of us, for teens it is ancient history.

Nevertheless, even though the classics are not mandated, teachers continue to assign them. Is it because they think English and language arts have to be about Hemingway, Melville, and Dickens? Or are they just not acquainted with the current high-quality books kids read on their own? Wonderful YA books address the same themes as the "classics" but are much more accessible to middle school readers. A foray into the world of YA books will assuage any lingering fears about offering kids choice in what they read.

We do not have to stick to same old, same old, in terms of what kids read. The ability to choose from among newer, more relevant titles is very powerful, and the middle schoolers I worked with took to it like ducks to water. We have the power to make a difference by rethinking our approach to exposing kids to good literature. I offer two simple formulas:

Equation 1: Books that kids choose and find relevant + A variety of titles and genres available = More reading.

Equation 2: More reading = Bigger vocabularies + More fluent readers + More knowledgeable kids.

READER PROFILE ▶ The Right Book in the Right Hands

In an otherwise noisy classroom, I notice one boy lost in *After Tupac & D Foster*, by Jacqueline Woodson (2008). When I ask him about it, he eagerly shows me the section he is reading. I tell him I love the book too, and Terrell says, "Yeah, Tupac is the greatest rapper of all time." Although the book is not the story of Tupac, his music is an important part of the lives of the three main characters, and Terrell is reading the book because Tupac's music is also important to him. How much time would he have spent trying to read *A Tale of Two Cities*? Would the experience have convinced him there are other good books out there he might like? *After Tupac & D Foster* engaged this boy with print. His classroom teacher suggested the book to Terrell because she knew he was a rapper. She wisely chose a book that worked for Terrell rather than force Terrell to work through a book he couldn't care less about.

Choice Meets the Developmental Needs of the Social Adolescent

Kids approaching adolescence are beginning to see themselves as autonomous. They want to control things more and more. It's a very frustrating period for them. Everything is controlled by their parents and others around them: the date and time of a dentist appointment, when they can get a ride to the mall, much of what they eat, what movies they can see. Yet the more chances kids get to control aspects of their lives, the more self-confidence they develop. Smart parents know that their child needs to begin to grow away from them, and they begin releasing the reins bit by bit. The resulting self-confidence translates to all aspects of the child's life.

In elementary school, students' days unfold in the same classroom with the same teachers and classmates. The teachers tend to be more nurturing, and the kids often have a fair amount of freedom when it comes to reading and learning. In contrast, middle school is all about being responsible and keeping notebooks for each class. Kids switch classes all day long, and teachers tend to impose fairly rigid discipline. Just when kids are looking for autonomy, they move into an environment that affords them less and less.

In many middle school language arts classrooms, what the kids read is entirely determined by the teacher, and in many cases the books are irrelevant or inaccessible. Two studies on reading motivation in high school students (Grigg et al. 2003; Levine et al. 1998) found that students (1) rarely read anything other than the textbook for instruction; (2) seldom collaborated with other students to interpret books; and (3) infrequently had the opportunity to choose a book on their own. Since we know that motivation for reading declines as social motivations increase (Otis, Grouzet, and Pelletier 2005), we need to latch onto students' need to connect with others. Reading can be shared with others in a variety of ways, not the least of which is talking about what we're reading. We need to change the balance of power in our classrooms and allow the kids to take the lead. Let them use materials other than the textbook (it's no secret how deadly boring they can be!). Why not encourage kids to surf the Internet or consult trade books to find out about a topic? Why not allow them to read and discuss books in groups, giving them the social interaction they crave? The more viewpoints, the more ideas shared, the more critical thinking kids will do. Along the way, their self-confidence about reading and contributing improves. This need not be a free-for-all. We still select the books in our classroom library, but the students have more freedom in deciding which ones they want to read and when they want to read them.

The in-common novel need not be avoided entirely. I am always looking for a way to get students discussing what they are reading, and an in-common novel is just the ticket. However, the three guiding principles apply here as well. For an in-common novel to be successful with students, it has to be one they can read, they should know a little about the topic, and it should be relevant to them. You will probably need to divide the class into three groups to accommodate the different reading levels, and when you see the difference that alone makes, you'll be eager to do it again. Some teachers do an in-common reading once during each grading period. Choose what works for you, but make sure kids discuss their reading as often as possible while still reading individually.

BOOKS KIDS ARE READING AND WHY

1. *Phineas Gage: A Gruesome but True Story of Brain Science*, by John Fleischman (2002). Nonfiction is compelling reading for this age group. And if it's a tad weird, even better! Phineas Gage was a real person who had the bad luck to have a railroad spike fly into the air and come down through his skull into the frontal lobe of his brain. Amazingly he was able to get up and walk home. Risking massive bleeding, doctors removed the spike, yet Phineas survived. Surely infection would get him in these days before antibiotics? Phineas lucked out again and the wound never became infected. But the damage to the frontal lobe was severe and his personality was forever affected. Kids are fascinated with the repercussions of frontal lobe damage; my students fought over who would get the book next. Truth, they say, is stranger than fiction, and kids' curiosity is piqued by Phineas Gage's story.

2. *Bone: Out from Boneville*, by Jeff Smith (2005). In *Out from Boneville* three cousins (what kind of creatures are they?) get separated in a vast, uncharted desert but are ultimately reunited. But evil lurks around the corner. What will happen to the Bone cousins? The book is part of relatively easy series of graphic novels. As a child Jeff Smith loved the cartoon format but wanted the length and breadth of a novel—hence the series. Reluctant readers in particular prefer a graphic novel over a thicker, all-words novel. While it can be argued that graphic novels are comic books in disguise, why is that a problem? Today's graphic novels are generally well written and compelling, and the art is fantastic. They have all the requisites of a novel—a beginning, a middle, and an end, with a problem that needs a solution. And kids will read them! We need to expand our notions of what reading is and include formats that appeal to kids. I would rather have students reading the Bone books than not reading at all. If they are reading, they can attempt other genres when they're ready.

3. *Knucklehead: Tall Tales and Almost True Stories About Growing Up Scieszka*, by Jon Scieszka (2008). It doesn't get more relevant than this, especially for middle school boys. Scieszka has tapped into his own boyhood and written this autobiographical collection of short stories that crack kids up. The individual stories are short and there are photographs and period illustrations throughout. The reading level is on the easy side for middle schoolers, so even weaker readers can be successful. They better not hog the book, though, or those proficient readers may just gang up on them!

4. The Twilight Saga, by Stephenie Meyer (various dates). I won't go into detail about this series, because everyone on the planet seems to have read it (or seen the movies based on it). Like the Vladimir Tod series, the Twilight books are a grabber for teens. It's boy-meets-girl with a twist. Bella meets Edward in her new school and is immediately drawn to him. She soon learns that Edward has a secret; he is a vampire. Will Bella stay away from Edward or throw caution to the wind? She could end up a vampire herself!

5. *Dog at the Door*, by Ben Baglio (Animal Ark series, 2002). Written on about a fourth-grade level, this book can be used in grades four through eight. Mandy's parents own a veterinary practice called Animal Ark. When a golden retriever appears on their doorstep one night, Mandy is determined to find out who its owners are. Kids with an interest in animals will gravitate toward the other books in this series as well. All contain real facts about the animals, which makes them even more engaging.

6. *The Lightning Thief*, by Rick Riordan (Percy Jackson series, 2005). A great opportunity to learn painlessly, *The Lightning Thief* is almost subversive in how it embeds great information about mythology in a book filled with amazing adventures and wizardry. I remember having to read Edith Hamilton's *Mythology* in school; mythology is inherently exciting, but I found it dead boring. Riordan kicks the action up a notch by making his protagonist a demigod (a son of Poseidon) and bringing in all the mythological gods that serve the book's plot. I recently met a precocious third grader who has read the whole series and drives her family mad by constantly spouting information about the Greek gods at the dinner table.

7. *Pop*, by Gordon Korman (2009). What we bring to what we read is the greatest help to our comprehension. Having some knowledge of a topic before one reads provides the schema on which to hang new information. What kids take away from their reading depends on their background knowledge or the background knowledge we give them. *Pop* deals with a timely topic—football and the effect on the brain of the repeated head injuries football players receive. Marcus meets an older man at the park who is willing to run some football plays with him and is surprised by how good the man is. He turns out to be an ex-NFL player now suffering from Alzheimer's disease triggered by all the blows to the head he took when he played. The book raises the issue of whether playing football is worth the risk of future brain dysfunction. One of the students I worked with, a football fan, knew a lot about this issue, and the things he shared prompted a lot of discussion and gave his classmates a lot of new knowledge.

8. *Stolen*, by Lucy Christopher (Printz Honor Book, 2010). In this contemporary realistic novel, Gemma is traveling to Vietnam with her art dealer parents when she is abducted in the Bangkok airport and spirited away to the Australian desert. Ty, her kidnapper, terrifies her at first, and the reader feels her fear. Over time, however, things shift and Gemma begins to see Ty in a new light. Is she identifying with her captor? Does she want to get away? This psychological novel is an absolute page-turner. The book will keep teen readers sitting on the edge of their seat. They can imagine being in a similar circumstance, so reading on to find out what happened is inevitable.

9. *The Invention of Hugo Cabret*, by Brian Selznick (2007). This huge book (533 pages) is a form unto itself. I like to call it the biggest book a reluctant or struggling reader will ever read. What makes it special is that so many of those 533 pages are drawings. The text is limited and manageable, and much of the story is conveyed through the art. The movie based on it, directed by Martin Scorsese, increases its popularity.

10. *Peak*, by Roland Smith (2008). Roland Smith is a reliable author for middle school readers. He writes great adventure stories, and this one is no exception. Peak is the main character's name; his father is a famous mountain climber who is off climbing Mount Everest. Peak gets arrested for scaling a skyscraper and is sent off to Mount Everest to join his father. There he gets to know his father in a way he never dreamed. Of course, very few (if any) middle schoolers have climbed Everest, but they can imagine themselves doing so. It's why Gary Paulsen's Hatchet books are also very popular.

LAST WORDS

What we know about children and their reading habits differs sharply from how we have traditionally taught reading in schools. The approach of choosing books from an outdated, archaic canon of "classics" and expecting students to read them seems permanently entrenched. Never mind that almost all these classics were targeted for adults when they were written—they are classics and should be read no matter the age or reading level. As a result our classrooms are full of disengaged readers who do everything they can not to read the boring books forced upon them, books that are often too difficult, that are irrelevant to their lives, and about which they have no background knowledge. It's no surprise that students shun school reading like the plague.

You can change all this by turning these negatives into positives. Find books that your kids can read and that are relevant to their lives, allow them to choose which of those books they will read, and give them the necessary background knowledge when appropriate. These changes will alter the face of reading in your classroom. Even students who dread reading will find themselves drawn to books. They will do what they most need to do to get better at reading—they will read. You, as the teacher, are happy, and so are your students. It's a win-win!

Setting the Stage

VOICE: ONE WAY TO MAKE READING REAL AND MEANINGFUL

I don't think I ever understood fully what "voice" meant to writing until I read Jack's piece for this book. If you want to know why kids want to read his books and why they get into his characters so thoroughly, you are in for a treat. Jack's characters absolutely become part of your world when you read one of his books. I still have Joey Pigza's voice in my head, and I read those books some time back. His latest novel, *Dead End in Norvelt*, won the 2012 Newbery Award, and I can't help but think that voice had a heck of a lot to do with it. Voice matters, first person matters, pulling kids in matters—and Jack Gantos is the master of it all.

FEATURED AUTHOR: Jack Gantos

It should come as no surprise that my books, so often written in the first person, depend on the "voice" of the character to narrate the story and wholly capture the reader. It is a vast task for the "voice" of the main character because not only does he or she have to supply the entire visually dense imaginative film of the novel, but the voice also has to deliver an equally compelling and essential "interior" landscape of each character. This dual task includes all the primary and subtle emotions, and all the motivations for the action, plus all the hopes, dreams, and intellectual puzzling of the characters. It is a busy labor for the "voice" and a labor that is filled with the peril of being too narrow in scope, which is why the first person has to be either generously expansive in his or her narrative rollout, or suggestively simple enough to coax the reader to fill in the blanks. This narrative balance is filled with dangerous tipping points, which is why I welcome the task, because when the "voice" works properly it reaches out of the text and thoroughly captures the reader.

Let's take my primary first-person "voices" to date: "Jack Henry" in the five volumes of Jack Henry short stories. "Joey Pigza" in the four volumes (a fifth to follow and complete the series), "Jack Gantos" in *Dead End in Norvelt*, "Ivy" in *The Love Curse of the Rumbaughs*, and "Jack Gantos" again in the memoir, *Hole in My Life*. (I have left "Rotten Ralph" out of this, as he is written from a third-person point of view—though he has a strong voice through his interior thoughts and self-revealing dialogue.)

The first-person voice speaks both directly and conspiratorially into the inner ear of the reader, with the result that it transforms the casual reader into a deeply empathetic reader who feels and sees all that the character feels and sees, and can join the character on the graphic stage on which the novel is revealed. The voice paints the human values of the heart and mind while also advancing the storyline. The first person also suggests the handshake and true bonding of writer to reader from the first sentence of the book, and that bond between writer and reader can be grafted in no other way. This establishes the trust the reader has in the writer and the responsibility the writer has to preserve this trust. When the first-person point of view is used with convincing precision, describing the external world of visual reality and the internal world of the heart and mind, then there is no other point of view that says to the reader, "Trust me—stick with me, and I will show you everything."

Chapter Two

VALUING WHAT KIDS VALUE

Making Reading Social and Meaningful

We know the basic needs of middle school readers. They want to read what they want to read, and they are drawn to books that reflect their own lives and interests. They don't want busy work and superficial worksheets that numb the brain (fill it out, hand it in, forget about it). They love to talk about books that captivate them. They want to share their reading experiences as much as they want to talk about playing the latest video game. The important thing is that their work in school be meaningful to them. Interacting with one another is something they love to do, and reading does have a social component.

How does this play out in a classroom?

OUR NEED TO SHARE EXPERIENCES

How often do we come out of a movie theater and then not talk about the film? Although we have been lost in a solitary experience in the darkened theater, our enjoyment of the movie does not end with the credits. It extends to the conversations we have with our friends about it afterward. We start in right away, discussing the plot, how good or bad the acting was, what a great story it was, connections with our lives. If we deem a character's decision a bad one, it's because we would not make that decision: we bring ourselves to the experience. This social interaction helps shape our appreciation of the movie. We need to share our experiences, and when we do, our understanding is almost always broadened.

It's the same with books.

Kids in middle school are burgeoning social creatures like no others. We know from psychologists like Piaget and Vygotsky that teens are trying to figure out who they are and who they are going to be. They are keenly aware of those around them, and more than anything else they want to fit in. Adolescents can be pretty annoying, with cell phones either glued to their ear or being manipulated by OMG- and BFF-texting fingers, but they are merely social animals. Anderman and Midgley (1997) have found that "the new focus on social and personal aspects of adolescent life seems to take precedence and reasons for attending school may rest more on being with friends than anything else." If adolescence is all about kids' social world, we need to harness that obsession and use it to our advantage in the classroom. If we can make reading a means for students to connect with their friends and peers, it will no longer be any kind of chore. Gone are (or should be) the days when we ask middle schoolers to work at their desks silently for extended periods. Let's get them interacting, sharing their opinions, and talking about books.

How Can Reading Be Social?
I Read All by Myself!

Under normal circumstances, we do read by ourselves. In class, students may employ partner reading and other communal comprehension strategies, but pulling words off the page is a solitary activity. Reading results from individual initiative and attention—we pick up a book and make our way through it to the end. Social interaction generally comes after we read. Not necessarily at the end of a book; it could be after a single chapter. In an article on the social aspect of reading, Guthrie et al. (1995) posit that interpersonal interaction in reading is a basic need and that if social interaction does not occur, students begin to feel isolated, alienated, or unnoticed and are then likely to feel frustrated. Frustrated students are not successful students, as we well know.

Davis (2003) says that social motivation promotes success in reading by providing a human safety net. Students who form close friendships have a sense of mutual trust in peers who will stand by them whether they succeed or fail, when they read something incorrectly or come up with a dumb idea. For middle school students who want only to fit in, this support system is critical. With their friends watching their back, risk-taking during discussion becomes that much easier.

Moving to a more collaborative teaching approach can be a little frightening. To field-test letting your class work collaboratively, see how they do with a picture book. Read the book aloud. Afterward, have groups of students (three or four are plenty) discuss a question you have preselected (a different question for each group). Have the groups choose someone to note their main points. Set a time limit if you like, perhaps five minutes. When time is up, ask each group in turn to read their question aloud and share the ideas they came up with. If you have not established a routine for this in your classroom, there may be some bumps in the road. Don't be deterred. Focus instead on what you hear from the students. Are their ideas thoughtful? I think you'll find your students get a lot more out of the book from the ideas they've bounced around.

A book I love for this purpose is *Passage to Freedom*, by Ken Mochizuki, illustrated by Dom Lee (1997). It is based on the experiences of Chiune Sugihara, a Japanese ambassador to Lithuania while Hitler was invading Eastern Europe. Lithuanian Jews came to Sugihara in droves, seeking visas to exit the country. To deny them a visa was to doom them to death at the hands of the Nazis. When Japan forbade any more visas, Sugihara, at great cost to himself and his family, continued to issue them. It is a story of bravery, standing up for what is right, and putting others before oneself.

Potential questions include:

1. The young son of Mr. Sugihara is telling the story. How do you think he felt about his father's actions? Why?

2. Disobeying orders from Japan and continuing to give out visas changed Mr. Sugihara's life in a number of ways. What are some of them?

3. Mr. Sugihara calls his family together to talk over the problem of the visas. Why? Wasn't it strictly a matter for the Japanese Consulate?

4. People are called on to do brave things when they least expect it. What are some ways in which Mr. Sugihara demonstrated bravery?

End by asking everyone in the class if she or he would do what Mr. Sugihara did.

Donna Alvermann (2001) cites Guthrie and Wigfield's take on the engagement model of reading as an effective approach to literacy instruction. Two aspects of that approach stand out for me:

1. *Student motivation.* Students need to have a sense that they can read the material successfully (self-efficacy), and teachers need to help them set

appropriate goals. Thinking reading is beyond you is a self-fulfilling prophecy.

2. *Social interaction.* There's that term again. Working with a partner on an experiment or discussing an idea in class with other students keeps students engaged and allows a variety of ideas to come forward.

Fostering engagement by motivating kids to read and using the social nature of reading as a means for doing so makes enormous sense. The most important thing we can do in the classroom to motivate and engage readers is discuss the books we read.

Reading Has to Be Meaningful

Social interaction is important, but so is meaningful reading. If kids don't see reading as meaningful, any motivation they may have had disappears. If we assign a novel and follow up with superficial activities that just take up class time and are the basis for a grade, kids turn off. They quickly learn how to play the game; engaged reading becomes a thing of the past.

READER PROFILE ▶ Making a Book Meaningless with Busy Work

When my son, Nick, moved to middle school he was placed in the language arts honors section. As spring break was approaching, his teacher assigned the 1974 Newbery Honor book *The Dark Is Rising*, by Susan Cooper. Nick dutifully read it and really enjoyed it. Although I am not a big fantasy fan, I read it as well and found it a well-written fantasy. When school reconvened, Nick and his classmates were given three sheets of activities (photocopied from a teacher activity book), each with a value assigned to it. Students could cobble together whatever activities they wanted as long as the values added up to an A, a B, etc. I looked over the activities and found nothing that would extend a child's understanding of the text. For example, Cooper has her main character drink a secret potion called *methglyn*. One activity option was to create a drink and bring it to class to share. I took Nick to the store, where we bought Hawaiian Punch, which he doctored with Worcestershire sauce and other weird ingredients and brought to school the next day. This wonderful story about good versus evil was reduced to making a silly drink. Since none of the activities meant anything to Nick, he barreled through enough easy ones to earn an A. In desperation, I asked how the discussions had gone, and Nick said the class never once talked about the book. Students just presented one inane activity after another. Then Nick said the saddest thing of all: "I hate that book." "No, you liked the book," I reminded him. "You hated what the teacher did to it." This teacher could have given her students a car repair manual and they would have gotten more out of it. Needless to say, these students were not keen on reading that whole year.

Some teachers like discussion, but only up to a point. They feel that they need to control the conversation and that there is only one right interpretation. One interpretation? Is there only one interpretation of Lois Lowry's multilayered *The Giver*? Even Lowry refuses to say what the book "means":

> *Many kids want a more specific ending to* The Giver. *Some ask me to spell it out. And I don't do that.* The Giver *is many things to many different people. People bring to it their own complicated sense of beliefs and hopes and dreams and fears. I don't want to ruin that for people who create their own endings in their minds.* (www.randomhouse.com/teachers/guides/give.html)

When readers finish reading this book about a utopian society that goes awry—a dystopia, really—the experiences they bring to it lead to a variety of interpretations. What do kids have to say about a utopia? What would a utopia look like to them? There is much to talk about in *The Giver*—and should they read *Animal Farm* at some later time, they will have a much better sense of it based on this earlier reading and discussion. Teachers who let kids talk about what they are reading know the conversation will zoom off in some pretty interesting directions. Kids bring up all kinds of ideas and become better thinkers because of it.

If the classroom climate emphasizes gaining meaning from big ideas, students are internally motivated to read and learn. For a teacher who is determined that learning will occur, they respond positively and go that extra mile. The sense that learning is valued encourages them to read deeply. Conversely, when kids see their teacher giving recall tests and worrying more about test scores than whether anything has been learned, kids no longer read and learn because they want to. They mirror the teacher's focus and read only for the test (Guthrie et al. 1995).

In an article in the *Journal of Adolescent & Adult Literacy*, Jewett, Wilson, and Vanderburg (2011, p. 416) discuss "talk" and meaning:

> *Dialogue provides readers with the means and opportunities to generate ideas and knowledge for their own uses and to question the author's point of view. It has the potential to lead readers toward diverse interpretations and more complex understandings of the text.*

They go on to say that dialogue (a.k.a. discussion) not only helps students learn about the text but also gives them opportunities to listen and respond to multiple voices and perspectives as they tease out individual and collaboratively built meanings. It is this give-and-take, this flexibility of thought, that teens respond to in the classroom. They are social readers, not solitary readers.

Discussing the theme of a book in small groups is beneficial to all group members. Adolescents yearn for social interaction, so playing this up is an instructional given. Arthur Applebee, the noted Stanford researcher on what works in English classrooms, has found that when teachers are able to build social interactions around course topics, students learn better. When students honestly exchange viewpoints about central points in literature, their achievement increases (Applebee et al. 2003).

When the teacher controls the questions and offers only one right answer, kids turn off. When kids are handed the reins and can control what they are reading and the ensuing discussions, they become involved. It's a win-win: they feel more connected to what they are learning, and they are getting the socialization they so deeply want. Not using their desire to connect and be social as they learn is a missed opportunity! Discussion is where real learning and real engagement take place.

If you are nervous about how a discussion will go (and many teachers are), look the book up online beforehand. Publishers often post discussion guides for teachers and, in general, they include strong questions that require critical thinking. Examine the questions and pull out the ones that will make your students think. Knowing you have a couple of questions at hand to jumpstart the discussion may make you feel a bit more comfortable.

In an end-of-year survey, I asked the WCMS middle school students what suggestions they had for improving reading in their classroom. One student said, "More time. More books, more group activities, more projects, more group projects." Excuse me? A student asking for more work? The variety and number of books in the classroom turned this student into a real reader who wants more books and more time to read them. Also notice that he likes interacting with other students and suggests more projects and more group-oriented activities. Interacting and sharing ideas is at the heart of being social, and using those social activities in our classrooms turns students on.

Blogger and sixth-grade teacher Sarah Mulhern has this to say about two students who both decided, on their own, to read *Gone*, by Michael Grant:

> *They talk about the book with each other and with me, coming to me to share their responses and exclamations. I LOVE IT! . . . It's amazing the power that social reading has. Why don't we harness this in more classrooms and use it? Students reading, recommending, and talking about books is more powerful than any literacy kit, basal reader, or literature set.* (thereadingzone .wordpress.com)

I love Sarah's enthusiasm at seeing what social reading means in her own classroom. She's dead right about harnessing this power and getting conversations about books started among students.

IF THEY CAN RELATE, THEY WILL READ IT

How do we use reading as a social activity to get kids reading? At our middle school we thought about this in two ways: (1) How can we help kids become active, not passive, in their reading and discussions? and (2) What kind of books will make them want to talk about what they are reading?

Enter author Jeff Kinney. Kinney had a great idea—he would write about that strange and befuddling creature, the middle schooler. All the trials and tribulations that Greg, his main character, suffers through revolve around the social nature of the middle school beast. All of us went through that awkward stage, suffering through one embarrassing situation after another, our faces sprouting new zits every other day. Why hadn't someone mined this stage of development before? Kinney even took it a step further, using a format (the diary) and an approach (humor) that hadn't been used much in books for middle school kids. He tells the story in a very funny way, appealing to readers' funny bones. Humor grabs kids this age in a big way. When something goes awry, they empathize and chuckle along. If kids in this awkward stage can laugh at themselves, there's hope for them, wouldn't you agree? Nerds are funny, and every class has them. Why not lay those cards on the table? Kinney's diary format puts us in Greg Heffley's head—we experience his ups and downs right along with him. The first-person voice is compelling, certainly, but the crux here is that the Diary of a Wimpy Kid books lay bare the underlying social scenarios that play out in these characters' lives every day. Middle schoolers live to make themselves noticed for great things and invisible for not-so-great things.

The Diary of a Wimpy Kid series didn't make the bestseller list because teachers said kids should read them. The most powerful recommendation kids can hear is one from their peers. If their buddies or BFFs think a book is cool, that's all they need to know. That kids talk about this series in and outside class speaks to how much fun the books are, how relevant they are to the kids reading them, how they absolutely nail the middle school experience, and how reading them is cool. You can't do much better than that.

The success of the Wimpy Kid series unleashed a deluge of emulators. While books like these may never reach the status of Melville's *Moby-Dick*, they are good choices to get kids reading. They show kids that there are appealing books out there. Who knows? They just might be something to look into! Remember my mantra: If students are reading, the chances I will be able to steer them toward more challenging books are good. If they are not reading at all, I have almost no hope of reaching them.

SOME POPULAR WIMPY KID LOOKALIKES FOR BOYS

Charlie Joe Jackson's Guide to Not Reading, by Tommy Greenwald (2011). Charlie Joe is not a big fan of reading. In fact, he does just about anything to avoid it. If he put half the energy into reading that he does into avoiding it, he'd be the most well-read middle schooler alive. The tips he gives on avoiding reading and the trouble they get him into makes this a fun book, especially for reluctant boy readers.

The Big Nate series, by Lincoln Peirce (various dates). Nate is a typically goofy sixth grader interested in anything but school. His nemeses, Gina the brainiac and the miserable Mrs. Godfrey, are a constant thorn in his side as Nate tries to be the awesomest kid in middle school.

The Strange Case of Origami Yoda, by Tom Angleberger (2010). Dwight may be the biggest dweeb on the planet—and in case anyone isn't sure of that, he has an origami Yoda puppet on his finger and gives out free advice in a pseudo Yoda voice. His classmates, who don't know what to make of this (other than Dwight is very weird), each contributes his or her thoughts on whether Dwight is channeling Yoda or has finally gotten weirder than anyone thought possible.

Darth Paper Strikes Back, by Tom Angleberger (2011). In this sequel to *The Strange Case of Origami Yoda*, Dwight's classmate Harvey has had enough of Origami Yoda and manages to get Dwight suspended. While Dwight's friends come up with wild reasons Dwight should return, Harvey and Darth Paper have other plans.

SOME POPULAR WIMPY KID LOOKALIKES FOR GIRLS

The Dork Diaries series, by Rachel Renée Russell (various dates). Nikki is starting a new school—a posh one—and wonders how she will fit in. She fits in but with all the drama a fourteen-year-old girl can muster. There are friendships, crushes, frustration, and lots of laughs.

The Popularity Papers series, by Amy Ignatow (various dates). This series adds a clever twist to the formula. Two friends, Lydia and Julie, decide to study the popular girls and understand what makes them popular. All does not work out as planned in these funny books about the nature of popularity.

Middle School Is Worse Than Meatloaf, by Jennifer L. Holm (2007). This very authentic book about middle school from a girl's point of view is illustrated with notes and lists that Holm's mother saved from the author's own middle school years.

LAST WORDS

Students in middle school are social by nature. Let's use this to our advantage by giving them books to choose from that have relevance to their lives and ensure that they have time to interact with their peers through activities and discussions. Through books like the Diary of a Wimpy Kid series, *The Strange Case of Origami Yoda*, and the Popularity Papers series, students who never read discover that there's something in books for them. These books nail the middle school experience perfectly, and kids learn that laughing at themselves may just be the ticket to survival. Kids relate to these books, talk about them, recommend them to one another, laugh about the situations in which the characters find themselves, and look for more books that help them navigate the often overwhelming world of middle school. If we want to make readers of these kids, showing them that there are books out there for them is the perfect starting point.

Once we hook them on these books we can easily coax them to try other books and other genres, thereby increasing the chances that reading becomes part of their daily life. Most important, though, we need to continue recommending books that are relevant and meaningful. We need to let them recommend books to one another since peer recommendations hold such weight with them. If we revert to archaic, boring books, we run the great risk they will lose interest. Most middle school readers would agree with noted reading scholar Frank Smith (1998), who argues that "reading is not a solitary activity." Readers are never alone. They join in the lives of the characters they are reading about. Touché.

Setting the Stage

LETTING KIDS' INTERESTS LEAD THEM INTO READING

I love to laugh every minute I can. Reading funny books tickles me no end. A recent auto-biography of the British actor Stephen Fry had me laughing out loud in a restaurant. Anything by Bill Bryson will bring about similar awkward moments. And absolutely anything by Jon Scieszka will have me cracking up, guaranteed. Jon Scieszka changed children's publishing in a big way when *The True Story of the 3 Little Pigs* was first published in 1989. Kids got the crazy humor and so did their teachers, which led to funny books finding a place in the classroom. Thank heavens.

But just as the Academy does not reward comedy films with Oscars, funny books aren't grabbing Newbery Awards at a fast clip either. Gordon Korman is one of the funny writers that kids love. He has a slew of funny books (as well as adventure and just about everything else), and middle schoolers eat them up. Both Jon Scieszka and Gordon Korman have made funny books a mainstay of middle school reading. It's all about letting kids read what they *want* to read.

Powerful nonfiction books can also pull kids in. Kids are drawn to insightful nonfiction that helps them make sense of the world around them. Susan Campbell Bartoletti's books tackle some of the topics that kids wonder about the most. Her books *Hitler Youth: Growing Up in Hitler's Shadow* and *They Called Themselves the K.K.K.: The Birth of an American Terrorist Group* do not disappoint. Booktalk some nonfiction titles and you will be surprised how many takers you have.

FEATURED AUTHOR: Jon Scieszka

I owe my life to humor.

Humor fed me. Humor saved me. Humor made me.

Let me explain.

Dinner at the Scieszka house, a house of six boys, was often a competitive event. There was only so much food, so you had to have some kind of talent or trick to get that extra helping. My talent was being funny. I would tell a joke and then, while everyone was laughing, snag the last piece of chicken. Humor fed me.

Working as a first-year second-grade teacher, I thought I was being a good educator by slogging through the sequence of deadly dull short stories in our reading anthology textbooks. My second graders grew to hate reading period. "Why did we just read that?" and "Who cares?" were two of the more polite responses to required reading time. I was in danger of losing all of my readers. So out of desperation, I shelved the anthologies and we started reading stories that I liked. My class and I read funny stories by James Marshall, Daniel Pinkwater, Norton Juster, Roald Dahl. My kids begged for more reading periods. Humor saved me.

When I took off from teaching to try to write kids' books, I wrote with the inspiration I had learned from my experiences in the classroom. I wrote to try and reach that kid in the back row who didn't think this reading stuff could be anything they were interested in. I wrote humor. I wrote the *True Story of the 3 Little Pigs*. I wrote the *Stinky Cheese Man and Other Fairly Stupid Tales*. I kind-of-suddenly had a career as a guy who writes funny kids' books. And then the Library of Congress named me the nation's first Ambassador of Young People's Literature. Me. The guy who writes funny books. Humor made me.

Scientists have studied humor. And some of them have even come up with reasons why humor is something we should value. But I think the best description of humor and why we should read it came from a third grader who described to me why he liked my story "The Really Ugly Duckling." He said, "You see, it's kind of like you have to know one thing—the story of the Ugly Duckling. Then you get the second thing—your story that's almost the same, but different. And together they make a third thing. And that just kind of lights up my whole brain. And I like that."

Humor is good.
Humor is valuable.
Reading humor can light up your whole brain.
And I like that too.

The Dead Dog Factor

I was a decent reader as a kid, but also somewhat disgruntled, and very hard to please. The books I loved best—also, come to think of it, TV shows, movies, and just about everything—were funny. I find it utterly baffling that humor isn't a larger part of a child's education. Consider for a moment your adult life: What do you use more often—your sense of humor, or your ability to recognize foreshadowing? Now look at the curriculum in your school district. Lots of foreshadowing; plenty of iambic pentameter. Humor? Not so much.

It's weird that we teach students every skill under the sun, yet many educators act as if a sense of humor is something you have to be born with, period. You hear it around the coffee pot in every faculty room: "The jokes are passing miles over their heads," or "My kids are way too literal to understand that kind of humor." Well, they didn't understand how to diagram sentences either until someone showed them how to do it! I didn't laugh at *Seinfeld* or *Monty Python* the first time I saw those shows. A sense of humor is like a muscle. It develops through *use*. Look at the novel studies students in your school district complete between, let's say, the fourth and eighth grades. I'll bet the total of funny books is less than the number that contain a single, relatively narrow plot point—a beloved dog dies. Think about that—we are sending kids to high school who, in their literary experience, have attended canine funerals more often than they have laughed. This was the inspiration for *No More Dead Dogs*. While kids may not always be the subtlest thinkers, they consistently manage to surprise us. When the kid in the back row with the faux-hawk and the total-warfare scowl sees the book cover with the award sticker and the golden retriever, it doesn't take him very long to figure out that the dog is living on borrowed time.

I don't mean to pick on the dead dogs. Many—most—of those novels are wonderful. What I object to is the amount of curriculum real estate they occupy, while humor languishes in the margins, if it's anywhere. This is a disservice to all our students; to reluctant readers, it might as well be a KEEP OUT sign. This reading thing is not for you.

It's true that relatively few young readers, when asked to identify a favorite genre, will choose funny books. The power of humor is in the breadth of its audience. Kids' tastes are very specialized—there are romance aficionados, fantasy nuts, mystery addicts, science fiction fans, steampunks, historical fiction lovers—the list goes on and on. But just about everybody likes to laugh.

FEATURED AUTHOR: **Susan Campbell Bartoletti**

Why do I write nonfiction for middle school readers?

When I was in seventh grade, the subject I liked least was history class. I didn't like to read the textbook. I didn't like to take notes. I didn't like to pay attention in class. I didn't like to study for tests.

I loved the library. There, I feasted on all sorts of nonfiction about historical events and subjects. I loved to read about the American Revolution, the Civil War, World War I and II. I read about the Pilgrims and the Puritans, the Westward movement, slavery, and biographies of famous people.

Go figure. The girl who didn't like history class loved to read about history. Perhaps my former history teachers wouldn't be surprised that someone who liked to read as much as I did grew up to become a writer. I'll bet they are surprised that I write about history.

Today, when I write nonfiction, I'm writing for the girl who loved facts wrapped in story and who loved to step out of time and travel to a place far removed from her normal, everyday existence.

I am also writing for the girl who liked to learn new ideas and perceptions and challenge authority. I am writing for the girl who liked to push limits and pursue an idea as far as she could. I am writing for the girl who loved facts.

As a writer, I understand it's important to engage young readers, and to do that, I write a form of literary nonfiction best described as narrative. Simply put, I take the facts of nonfiction and wrap them in story.

The art and craft of writing nonfiction for young readers requires as much skill and imagination as the writing of fiction. For me, the difference is this: When I write historical fiction, I take the facts of history and filter them through my imagination in order to write a story that could have happened, based on the facts.

When I write nonfiction, however, I must never invent. Every fact, every detail, every word of dialogue, must be accurate and verifiable. (Of course, I can argue that providing accurate information should be the goal of all authors.)

As a nonfiction writer, my goal is to write true stories that engage the reader. For me, engagement begins with the story germ. (That's what the novelist Henry James called the ideas that he would grow into a story or novel.)

For nonfiction, my germs are true stories. The germ might be a subject I like or know. It might be an idea I don't know or don't understand and want to explore further.

No matter what sort of germ it is, one thing remains true: the idea must turn my heart over and compel me to rush to the library to learn more. (The research process often takes a year or two or even longer. It's this stage that gives the story its muscle and tissue and bone.)

Ultimately, it's the writing that breathes the story to life. To quicken the story, I use the same literary devices that fiction writers use: setting, character, dialogue, scenes, plot (rising-and-falling action), plotting turns, vivid writing, and more— all the while pledging to tell a true, accurate story. I repeat my mantra: I Must. Not. Invent.

Middle school teachers have a tough job. Like the writer, they must engage their students. Some days it's easy; other days it's the hardest work you'll ever love. But don't give up on kids like me who may not like history class! Keep the nonfiction coming.

Chapter Three

FINDING THE RIGHT BOOK FOR THE RIGHT READER

It's Easier Than You Think!

Some years back Gary Paulsen's pivotal book, *Hatchet*, was the target of censorship in my elementary school. A teacher used it with a book group in her fourth-grade classroom, and a parent, who claimed the book frightened her son, was adamant that it be removed from the elementary, middle, and high school libraries in our district. I was surprised that the book, which appeals to so many boys and helps them connect with books, affected her son the way it did. Of course, if a book is unsettling for a child, he should never be forced to read it. That's common sense. But that shouldn't mean other students *can't* read it.

Concerned teachers spent a lot of time and effort defending the book and formed committees to read and discuss the book. I too fought the ban, first because I have a personal distaste for censorship but also because the book was such an important tool in my arsenal for getting boys to read. They could imagine themselves stranded just like Brian, with only a hatchet between themselves and death. They could stare down every threat, whether a moose or a raging storm. They could survive! (Or so they thought. My guess is they wouldn't last a day without their cell phones and Xboxes, but I could be wrong.)

The issue eventually made its way to the school board. The board president objected to the book, but fortunately he was in the minority, and *Hatchet* remains on the shelves of the school libraries. As Shakespeare said, all's well that ends well.

I mention this episode for three reasons:

1. Kids' development—where they are in their maturity—impacts enormously what they want to read. It goes back to relevance but also to their sense of themselves, their identity.

2. It exemplifies the gender issues that arise in the classroom every day. Gender has to be one of the issues we address (though not the only issue) in providing a wide range of books.

3. In moving away from anthologies and textbooks, how do we know which books are age appropriate and suitable for our students?

These can be stumbling blocks for teachers, but they needn't be. There are easy ways to become comfortable with our book selections.

Recognizing Increasing Maturity

Talk about psychological development may seem somber, but it is a big part of knowing which books to match with which kids. Once we know where the children in our class are developmentally, we can choose appropriate books for them.

Hatchet is intended for readers aged ten and older. This guideline isn't arbitrary; it's the age at which children begin dealing with the issues explored in the book, which in large part have to do with survival. Third graders aren't thinking about survival and living a life away from their parents, they're just hoping they get invited to their best friend's birthday party on Saturday! Ten-year-olds, on the other hand, are beginning to see themselves as one day being on their own. Although not yet able to fend for themselves in the real world, they know the necessity of doing so is coming. In this book they meet Brian Robeson, age thirteen, the only passenger in a small plane that crashes when the pilot has a fatal heart attack. Brian survives the crash but has to find ways to survive deep in the woods and completely alone. Adolescents are drawn to this story because they are wrestling with similar issues as they begin to break free of their parents. Although they are not fending off moose and mosquitoes, they *are* building a new world for themselves. Brian's successes and failures are their successes and failures.

Children in sixth through eighth grade are moving from Piaget's *concrete operational stage*, during which they master logical thinking, to his *formal operational stage*, during which they become capable of hypothetical reasoning and problem solving. They can look at a character's situation, recognize the inherent problem, and form an opinion of the character based on what the character decides to do. They are able to see Brian's problems—in addition to being stranded in the wild, he is dealing with his parents' divorce—as their own and work out what needs to be done. Paulsen has said he put the issue of divorce in the book because most kids will not have to survive in the wild but will have to survive divorce. Tweens and teens notice that Brian's trials help him put the divorce in perspective when he returns home. A third grader would not have that perspective. It takes the flexible thought processes of a teen to weigh all the possibilities and know what makes sense for that character. Like Brian, teens are trying to figure out who they are and how they fit in. They are the character.

RESPONDING TO AN EVOLVING MORAL COMPASS

Adolescents' moral stance is changing as well. Psychologist Lawrence Kohlberg developed a framework delineating how children change in their moral development as they mature (1981). He places teens at the conventional morality stage. That is, they believe that the community dictates what its expectations are and its members are supposed to behave in that way. Good behavior means following the community's expectations; acting on the basis of good intentions; and demonstrating love, empathy, trust, and concern for others. In *Hatchet*, Brian sees his mother as letting the community down when she kisses a man who is not his father. Only over time does he realize there may have been reasons justifying her behavior. This is a perfect time to be sharing books that feature issues kids can think through and examine their own feelings about. Moral dilemmas make for rich conversations with kids in grades 6–8. They are beginning to think much more critically and can discuss alternative sides of arguments for the first time.

Priscilla Cummings' *Red Kayak* (2004) is a wonderful book centered on a moral dilemma. Brady, the narrator, gets caught up in a situation that begins in the gray area between right and wrong but quickly becomes black as night. An example of a booktalk on *The Red Kayak* is shown in the following box.

Framing a Moral Dilemma Through Booktalks:
An Example for Teachers

Red Kayak by Priscilla Cummings (2004)

- *Begin by identifying the moral dilemma.* In this book, exactly what happened is revealed piecemeal to the reader. But we know that the big problem is that two of Brady's friends went too far with revenge and a child lost his life. The real moral dilemma is not about the bad choices these boys made. Rather, it is about how Brady decides to act when he learns what his friends did.

- *Craft a booktalk: part summarization, part "what if."* The booktalk has to tell some of the story to set the stage and entice the readers in, but it should *not* be a summary. Once the kids know what's going to happen, they have no reason to read the book. Instead, build them up so that they are dying to know what happens and give them some possibilities of how it might turn out. Pose these possibilities as questions so that they see them as questions and begin to construct their own sense of what has happened and what should be done. Never give the ending away or you have lost your reader.

- *Discuss at the outset.* Talk about the questions you just posed. If something bad happens that was completely unintentional but occurred as a result of your actions, are you culpable? These big questions help students begin to think deeply about what they are about to read. They now have the big ideas in their minds as they enter the story. You can bet those questions are going to influence what they get out of that book. It's a lot like asking someone to forget about an elephant in the room. Once you mention it, you don't forget it. This helps focus them as they read.

How the Booktalk Might Look

Brady and his two buddies, Digger and J.T., are not happy about how their fishing town on the Chesapeake Bay is changing. McMansions are popping up everywhere filled with people who don't see their community in the same way that their own families have. Digger is particularly ticked off because his grandfather's place has been sold and no longer looks anything like the place he knew.

The new owner goes out in a kayak with her young son when the bay is choppy and the current swift, and Brady feels guilty that he didn't warn her of the dangers.

When they find the kayakers' overturned vessel and the young boy dies, Brady is guiltier than ever.

What made the kayak sink? Was it the conditions on the bay that day? Was it the woman's inexperience in a kayak or was it Brady's fault for not warning her? Brady finds out that someone he knew actually tampered with the kayak's hull, making it unseaworthy. What should Brady do? On the one hand, the boys' feelings of anger and frustration over the newcomers changing their lives are very understandable. Does that make it all right to teach them a lesson? When vandalism causes a death, does it become murder? And what do you, as a friend, do about it when you know the truth? There's going to be no simple slap on the wrist for the culprit in this case, is there? Read *Red Kayak* to find out what Brady does in the end.

Booktalks with Picture Books

Powerful picture books can pack a moral dilemma into just a few well-chosen words and images. Consider using picture books to spark conversation and draw parallels with other books students are reading. A booktalk with a picture book looks a lot like the booktalk described above, but it could also include reading the *entire* book and concluding with a discussion of the book as a whole. At that point, everyone will have read the book and will have lots of oral ammunition to draw conclusions and bolster their arguments.

Identifying the theme you want the students to focus on in a book takes practice. Here's another example of my thought process when I get ready to present a book to kids.

To open a unit on diversity I choose the picture book *Smoky Night*, by Eve Bunting (1994). It's the story of a young boy and his mother who live in a neighborhood that is in flames during the Los Angeles riots of 1992. The neighborhood is diverse, and there is a deep-seated distrust among the different ethnicities until they are forced to rely on one another that night to get to safety. When they all wind up in a shelter overnight, friendships are forged and the distrust melts away.

What do I want my students to take away from this book? I don't want to talk specifically about the riots or the police brutality toward Rodney King that started the whole mess, although another teacher might very well want to talk about these serious issues. Why riots erupt is a great conversation to have with kids. What underlying problems lead to a riot? This is also a great book to read to begin a discussion on prejudice or cliques or individuality.

But I want to use this book to get kids thinking about seeing beyond differences and realizing that the things human beings have in common are far more plentiful than our differences. It's about breaking down barriers and getting to know individuals. My questions will direct them there.

TRY IT OUT

Identifying a Theme

Read one or two books from the list below and see whether you can tease out the theme you would like your students to center on while they are reading. Choose a title, identify a theme, and plan how you might use it with your students:

1. *Faithful Elephants: A True Story of Animals, People and War*, by Yukio Tsuchiya, illustrated by Ted Lewin (1988). During World War II, it was feared that the animals in the Tokyo Zoo would escape during a bombing raid and threaten the citizens of Tokyo. To avoid this, all of the animals considered dangerous were killed. It was not easy to kill the beloved elephants.

2. *Freedom Summer*, by Deborah Wiles, illustrated by Jerome Lagarrigue (2001). Two boys, one black and one white, in Mississippi in 1964 find that even though the Civil Rights Act has been passed, there are always some people who will not change their views.

3. *The Araboolies of Liberty Street*, by Sam Swope, illustrated by Barry Root (1989). General Pinch likes everyone to follow rules—his rules. His most important rule is that every house on Liberty Street must look exactly the same. But then the Araboolies move in and everything changes.

4. *Wangari's Trees of Peace: A True Story from Africa*, by Jeanette Winter (2008). Wangari Maathai was certain that the deforestation of Kenya was undermining the lives of her fellow countrymen. Maathai educated the populace and led them to replant the woodlands, which had far-reaching effects for their country. Maathai won a Nobel Peace Prize for her herculean efforts.

5. *Nettie's Trip South*, by Ann Turner, illustrated by Ronald Himler (1987). Nettie takes a trip down South on the eve of the Civil War and sees firsthand the plight of the slaves, which she finds incomprehensible.

6. *Passage to Freedom: The Sugihara Story*, by Ken Mochizuki, illustrated by Dom Lee (1997). Chiune Sugihara was a Japanese diplomat in Lithuania in 1940 when Hitler was invading the country. Sugihara wanted to issue visas to those Jews who wished to leave Lithuania, but his government forbade it. With his family's blessing, Sugihara disregarded the Japanese government's directive and issued thousands of visas, saving thousands of Jewish lives.

7. *Teammates*, by Peter Golenbock, illustrated by Paul Bacon (1990). When Jackie Robinson came up from the Negro baseball leagues and joined the Brooklyn Dodgers, not everyone approved. Fans taunted him, and his team-mates were less than accommodating. Robinson wasn't fully accepted until Pee Wee Reese took a stand and declared Robinson was his teammate.

8. *Wilma Unlimited: How Wilma Rudolph Became the World's Fastest Woman*, by Kathleen Krull, illustrated by David Diaz (1996). Wilma Rudolph, an African American from Clarksville, Tennessee, overcame enormous obsta-cles, including life-threatening, crippling polio, to become the first woman to earn three gold medals in the 1960 Olympics in Rome, Italy.

USING HUMOR AS MOTIVATION

All our book choices don't have to feature deep moral issues. First and fore-most, kids' reading experience should be fun. Yes, we want them to develop as critical thinkers and be able to draw inferences, but ultimately we want them to love books. That means giving them a wide range of books, even (maybe especially?) ones that crack them up. Humor is a good thing. Kids love to laugh and are drawn to joke and riddle books in the early grades—the simplest riddle or joke can send them into gales of laughter. They share their jokes, and we chuckle along while groaning inside. But if kids are laugh-ing, they are enjoying what they are reading.

Humor is an opportunity to get kids reading. Start with Dr. Seuss, move on to the books of Jim Marshall, then to Jon Scieszka and Lane Smith's *The True Story of the 3 Little Pigs*, and wind up with *Captain Underpants*. Scieszka's *Knucklehead: Tall Tales and Almost True Stories of Growing Up Scieszka* is a good example of a book appropriate for kids in grades 6–8 that also tickles their funny bone. Each time I read aloud from this collection of hilarious stories in classrooms, kids beg for it to be added to their class library.

Since anecdotal evidence is always looked down upon, I've searched for empirical data—and there are some! Paul McGhee and his colleagues have explored humor as a motivational tool and found a clear connection between humor and the brain. In *Humor: Its Origin and Development* (1979) they iden-tify four stages of humor development and find, not surprisingly, that they correspond with the cognitive development theories of Piaget. Understand-ing and creating humor are cognitive skills. Anyone who has paid attention to a *Seinfeld* episode knows that a good comedian takes something ordinary and twists it into the extraordinary. That requires serious brainpower. P. Y. Chik (2005), while teaching sixth-grade English language learners in Hong Kong, investigated whether students were motivated to read by humor. She found that humorous English reading material produced statistically significant changes in students' intrinsic and extrinsic motivation. Her students developed stronger intrinsic motivation and relied less on extrinsic motivation when they were allowed to read humorous books.

My experience tells me that funny books draw kids in, but now I can also cite research showing that funny books motivate kids to read. Bring on *Knucklehead*! Boys, in particular, are drawn to this book. It's funny, irreverent, and features all kinds of silly and gross things that are right up boys' alley.

Does Gender Affect Reading? You Better Believe It!

Boys and girls are different in so many ways (*vive la différence!*), but the majority of teachers do not take those differences into consideration when choosing books for their classroom. In general, boys tend to be more hands on and active in everyday life, while girls tend to be less boisterous, more considered in their approach, and more emotional (Newkirk 2002). It isn't surprising then that these two groups want different reading material. Reading preferences mirror one's nature.

Boys tend to prefer books with a lot of action and adventure, like Anthony Horowitz's *Stormbreaker* (2001). In this novel, Alex Ryder finds out that the uncle he has been living with in London has died in a car crash. But when he goes to see the car in a wrecking yard, he finds the car riddled with bullet holes. This was no car crash—his uncle was murdered! It turns out that his uncle was a spy for England's well-known intelligence agency, MI6, and the agency wants Alex to join their ranks. The suspense and intrigue are exactly what boys look for in entertainment—immediate engagement that keeps them hooked—and this book (and the series it spawned) supplies it.

Girls, on the other hand, like books that are more heartfelt and even romantic. They are willing to allow time for characters to develop, and if a tear should be shed in the process, all the better. Emily, a fifth grader, read *Bridge to Terabithia*, by Katherine Paterson (1977), and truly mourned when the character Leslie died. She liked getting a sense of that feeling of loss. She later asked me, "Where do you keep the sad books?" as if libraries had a special section for them. Emily went on to middle school and luxuriated in every

Lurlene McDaniel book she could get her hands on (McDaniel's books all revolve around a tragedy in which someone dies).

READER PROFILE ▶ A Good, Scary Romance

Alexis is a middle school student who enrolled in our summer reading program in rural Virginia to get some extra help over the summer. She does not see herself as a reader and makes sure we know it. (Kids who aren't readers often tell you they aren't interested in reading as a way of protecting themselves. When they fail miserably, they can say, "See, I told you so.") Our summer program moved away from the conventional tutoring model with a structured hour of reading and rereading, with a bit of word study and comprehension work thrown in. The focus is on getting kids to read. Our goal is to connect these kids with books, so we give book talks on a number of compelling, somewhat edgy young adult titles. Alexis chooses *I Heart You, You Haunt Me*, by Lisa Schroeder (2008), because she is drawn to this story of a teenage girl, Ava, whose boyfriend, Jackson, has died. He comes back as a ghost to help her deal with his death and release her from any promises they made. Written in free verse, the book is accessible for reluctant readers like Alexis, and the romantic storyline pulls them in. The next morning Alexis arrives beaming, holding up her book. "I read this whole book last night, and I'm not a reader." "Yes, you are a reader," I counter—a compliment she accepts. For the remainder of the program, Alexis reads every day. She has discovered that there are books out there for her and is psyched that she found them. (Lisa Schroeder has two more books in the same vein: *Far from You* and *Chasing Brooklyn*. Guess what Alexis reads next?)

READER PROFILE ▶ A Book on Baseball Hits It out of the Park

Tyler is a tough nut to crack. He has been tutored all year before coming to the summer program, and he makes it clear that reading equals torture as far as he is concerned. Every day when he arrives he says, "I only have to be here an hour, right?" Throughout the session his eyes seldom stray from the clock. At intervals he announces, "Forty more minutes," "Thirty more minutes," "Twenty more minutes." After listening to a number of booktalks, Tyler chooses *Shakespeare Bats Cleanup*, by Ron Koertge (2003), which is also written in free verse. Tyler is a baseball nut, so the topic appeals to him, and free verse looks less daunting than regular prose. By the next day he's read half the book and apologizes for not having finished it (he had a ballgame to play the night before). When the program ends three weeks later, Tyler tells us he's sorry it's over. Is this the same kid who counted every minute of the first few hours he was with us?

Working with Alexis and Tyler (see the reader profile boxes), we didn't assume Alexis would choose a romantic story and Tyler would choose a baseball theme. We offered a wide array of choices and left it to them. In a pivotal book on boys and literacy, *Reading Don't Fix No Chevys* (2002), Michael Smith and Jeffrey Wilhelm sum up the research on gender differences. Knowing the reading likes and dislikes and the learning styles of both boys and girls will only help us find the books that will hook them.

Smith and Wilhelm found that girls start reading early, while boys lag behind (and tend to stay behind, since they read less than their female peers). National Assessment of Educational Progress (NAEP) scores have consistently ranked boys lower than girls in reading since they started testing in 1992. While boys have managed to raise their scores little by little over the years, they still remain behind their female counterparts in the most recent published results (National Center for Education Statistics 2009). The gap is real and it remains to this day. Offering a wide variety of books that are relevant to both boys and girls is a way to begin to reverse that trend.

Reading widely allows students to understand how narrative and expository texts work, which in turn means they comprehend more, so it's no surprise that girls outdo boys in comprehension in both genres. Boys, however, tend to be better at finding information. Boys also tend to see themselves as inadequate or even as nonreaders, and they don't care as much about reading as girls do. They have a poor sense of their own reading prowess and it gets worse as they age: nearly 50 percent of all boys see themselves as nonreaders by high school.

Boys' attitudes toward reading are dispiriting, and those attitudes are reinforced by the books they are forced to read in school. Teachers unintentionally stack the deck against them. When I discovered this research, I vowed I would never let a boy's self-deprecating comment about his reading skills go by without offering an encouraging rebuttal.

Boys and girls read different things. Boys are more inclined to read informational texts while girls read more fiction. Boys' reading tends to gravitate toward magazines, newspaper articles, graphic novels and comic books, and texts on hobbies and sports, and they really enjoy escapism (science fiction or fantasy) and humor. They like reading electronic texts more than girls do as well. One of the funniest characteristics about boys' reading is that they resist reading stories about girls ("Why would I want to read about a girl?"), afraid they'll be seen as girlish if they read a story with a female protagonist. They have little in common with girls and therefore reading about one seems utterly pointless. Girls, however, are happy to read books with a male protagonist. A book like Shiloh won't put them off despite the young boy pictured on the cover.

Knowing all this we still offer a book like *Little House on the Prairie* for boys to read when (a) they are not drawn to fiction, (b) it has girl characters almost exclusively, (c) it's not particularly humorous, and (d) it's not about something they can picture themselves doing. Knowing that boys and girls like different things can help inform our choice of the reading material (fiction, nonfiction, magazines, graphic novels) we offer.

Smith and Wilhelm also found that boys and girls differ in how they respond to what they read. While girls certainly choose books based on their covers (most of us do), the cover and appearance of a book are very important to boys. Boys are less likely to discuss a book in class; they prefer active responses, not sitting and talking—responses that require more of a teacher's time. These are the very behaviors that drive teachers crazy! Sadly, boys tend to get called out and criticized for their dodgy reading and writing. With all of these things going on, it's a wonder any boys read.

Next time we're ready to blow our tops, think about how hard it is for boys *not* to "misbehave." What we see as disruptive, they see as normal behavior. Let's harness that energy and come up with ways to have boys respond to what they read in an active rather than a passive way. Most important, as with any child, we shouldn't criticize them but instead point out what they are doing right in their reading and show them how to build from where they are.

TRY IT OUT
Active Booktalk Alternatives

1. Give a small group of boys a graphic novel they'll want to read and let them deliver the booktalk as a rap. They will have to summarize the story, write a rap, and act it out. Middle school kids are all about not being a nerd, and rap is cool. They'll be so thrilled they don't have to write a "booktalk," they won't even realize that they're doing a booktalk disguised as a rap. You might share *Nathaniel Talking*, by Eloise Greenfield (1988), to help them see what the rap might look like. *Yummy: The Last Days of a Southside Shorty*, by G. Neri, illustrated by Randy Duburke (2010), is a graphic novel that will grab middle school boys and lends itself to a rap interpretation. It is in many ways a cautionary tale, the true story of a young boy nicknamed Yummy who, although only eleven years old, is part of a Southside Chicago gang. During a gang shooting, a stray bullet from Yummy's gun kills an innocent fourteen-year-old girl. The narrator, Yummy's fictional classmate, describes the last three days of Yummy's life. What went so wrong that Yummy ended up dead himself? When the boys finish the book you will definitely want to discuss this question.

2. Young adult literature with innovative and imaginative features and structures are great activity starters. *Charlie Joe Jackson's Guide to Not Reading*, and *Charlie Joe Jackson's Guide to Extra Credit* by Tommy Greenwald (2011/2012), will crack up all your middle school boys. Charlie Joe is determined to keep his streak of not reading going throughout middle school. His lists of tips on how to avoid reading are hilarious and resonate totally with middle schoolers. Have students "perform" the book by reciting the lists.

Of course the generalization that boys and girls have different tastes in the stories they read has exceptions. To give boys access only to a particular set of books and girls another does them an incredibly limiting disservice. There will always be girls who like a good car crash and boys who like a sad story. The last thing we should do is reinforce gender stereotypes. All books should be available to all kids. Let them decide what it is they want to read, but offer them the entire spectrum of what girls like and what boys like. The beauty of a well-told story is that it allows us to inhabit the life of another and try it on for size. It helps all readers, male and female, develop empathy for others and learn from the situations the characters find themselves in.

READER PROFILE ▶ Gender Differences Can Narrow the Audience

Some years ago now my son, Nick, asked me to recommend a book for him to read for fourth-grade class. His teacher had moved them into mystery and he was, as always, allowed to choose what he wanted to read. I recommended Avi's *The True Confessions of Charlotte Doyle*, but he wasn't interested in the slightest. I couldn't understand why he didn't take me up on my suggestion. Avi was a favorite writer of his with some great edge-of-your-seat books (*Wolf Rider*, *Windcatcher*, and *Something Upstairs*), but Nick wouldn't read this one because of the name "Charlotte" in the title. The next day his teacher, independent from me, suggested *The True Confessions of Charlotte Doyle* and Nick decided to read it. Apparently his teacher held more sway than old Mom did, but I was thrilled he was reading the book. He ended up loving it because it is a swashbuckling adventure that I knew he'd like. What could be more compelling than a locked-room mystery on a ship smack in the middle of the Atlantic Ocean? It took some coercion to get Nick past the title, but when he did he was glad he had. I'm betting, though, that even now in a bookstore he would gravitate to books that don't have a girl's name in the title.

If boys and girls have such different tastes in books and most teachers are women, the possibilities for misconnection are great. Most teachers picking out books for classroom reading are unaware of their gender bias. They choose good books they like, but too often they're books boys won't like. Many women like heartwarming stories; boys hope there's a car chase that ends in a fiery wreck. Two very different vantage points are at work here, and we need to be mindful of them. I was lucky. I had a principal early in my career who brought gender bias to my attention. I also saw firsthand which books brought the boys to the table and which ones kept them away. Mention *The Secret Garden* to your average third-grade boy and watch his face collapse in horror. Girls light up when they see it. Conversely, girls don't gravitate as strongly to *Captain Underpants*, but the series has started many a reluctant boy reading. Having said that, as a kid I would have delighted in *Captain Underpants* but also read *Little House on the Prairie* and loved it (so much that I wrote my own book based on the series when I was in third grade!). We need not pigeonhole kids as readers. Knowing kids' individual tastes and being aware of our own biases is the best way to offer kids books that speak to them.

WHAT *IS* READING?

Boys who don't consider themselves readers will still pore over the sports section of the paper, devour comic books, and read video game manuals from beginning to end. Because that kind of reading is not typically allowed in school, they don't see it as real reading. *We need to make sure they understand that reading informational books, magazines, and newspapers is reading.* We need to expand our definition of what reading is to include what interests them. It needs to include boy-friendly formats, as well as the incredibly varied graphic novels now being published. Today's teenagers have been exposed to visual media since birth. Their openness to story in a visual format is a good thing— and if it connects them to print as well, it's a great thing.

READER PROFILE ▶ Harrison and the Dirt Bike Magazine

I'm interviewing students about their reading habits. Harrison is engrossed in a dirt bike magazine. When he sees me, a defiant look crosses his face as if to say, *I dare you to tell me I can't read this.* I ask what he's reading, and his voice takes on an edge as he tells me he likes to read about dirt bikes. I respond that reading about what interests us is a great thing. His defiant look changes to suspicion. When I ask him what he likes about the magazine, Harrison tells me in great detail: information about interchangeable bike parts and new, more powerful technology; reviews of different models; and on and on. Harrison is a very real, very connected reader who is learning incredible things from a magazine that most of us would write off as pap. Not so, as Harrison proves to me. He is smart as a whip and devouring what he reads. It's wonderful to see such an

---

engaged reader. Later that day his teacher asks what I think of what Harrison was reading. I tell her I saw great things going on with him. He was engaged, he was learning a ton from the magazine, and he was enjoying every minute of it. I also suggest she might try to find some of Matt Christopher's books about dirt bike racing for Harrison so that he is exposed to narrative as well as expository. Harrison is a reader and will probably turn to print throughout his life. Isn't that what we are hoping for?

When purchasing books for the classroom libraries at Warren County Middle School (WCMS), we kept gender reading preferences in mind but our primary goal was obtaining books that were worth reading. Even though we wanted to include boy books and girl books, they had to be good books. We made sure there was a wide variety of fiction, nonfiction, magazines (for kids like Harrison), anthologies, poetry, and short stories. Having such a wide selection made a huge difference to these kids. One WCMS student suggested there should be "like two days of just reading in class." Again and again in end-of-year surveys the students asked for "more time to read" as a way to make class better.

Caveats Regarding Gender

While it is important to notice what kinds of books attract boy readers and girl readers, it is not the only way to match kids with books—it's a piece of the puzzle. There are some kids who break all the boundaries and read widely. Remember Terrell (see Chapter 1) who was reading *After Tupac & D Foster*? That book was all about girls. Terrell read it because he loved Tupac Shakur's rap music more than he hated reading about girls. For Terrell, it wasn't a gender thing, it was an interest thing.

Some books attract both genders. Suzanne Collins' *Hunger Games* series is one of them. In the first volume, a brave young girl, Katniss, manages to come out breathing in a fight-to-the-death survival game. The two sequels, *Catching Fire* and *Mockingjay*, follow her through many other spectacular feats, and readers are on the edge of their seat throughout. If a book has something for everyone, it will be read by both sexes. Boys will be drawn to the adventure in these novels as Katniss uses her survival skills and her smarts to stay alive. (It doesn't hurt that there are boy characters that Katniss partners with along the way.) Girls love the idea of the girl being the awe-inspiring winner, and they appreciate the slight hint of romance in the story. All in all, these books have something for everyone.

My intention in talking about gender is not to reinforce rigid gender stereotypes but rather to give kids a way to connect with what they read and help them think their way through the muddle of adolescence. However, there are books that reinforce negative stereotypes. One popular series for younger children known for its gender stereotyping is *The Boxcar Children*, by Gertrude Chandler Warner. In these books, the boys get to be adventurous and daring, while the girls are caretakers and happily putter around the kitchen fixing dinner. One of the things I've always liked about the Nancy Drew books is that Nancy Drew is anything but a stereotype. She is a girl sleuth who gets into risky situations but is capable of thinking her way out of them. She isn't sitting around at home darning socks and baking pies. She may wear a charming frock and pumps, but that girl rocks!

NONFICTION

Teens like nonfiction, especially if it is a bit gruesome. The nonfiction available for kids today is light-years away from the nonfiction I read as a child. The books are more accessible, better designed, wonderfully written, and often contain backmatter that steers kids in the direction of more information on the subject. There are photographs, maps and charts, glossaries, and definitions, all designed to have children learn as much as they can. Students don't even have to be able to read many of these books. The pictures and insightful captions offer information that is accessible for developing readers: perusing these books lets them feed their intellects even if they can't yet read every word.

KNOCKOUT NONFICTION

Amelia Lost, by Candace Fleming (2011). What happened to Amelia Earhart?

America Is Under Attack: September 11, 2001, by Don Brown (2011). A wonderful book about the attack on the twin towers in New York as well as the impact 9/11 has had on us as a people. Straightforward reporting with no sensationalizing.

Blizzard of Glass: The Halifax Explosion of 1917, by Sally M. Walker (2011). What's more interesting than a ship blowing up?

The Book of Blood: From Legends and Leeches to Vampires and Veins, by HP Newquist (2012). Vampires are always popular.

Bootleg: Murder, Moonshine, and the Lawless Years of Prohibition, by Karen Blumenthal (2011). Do kids today even know there was a time when alcohol was prohibited? They'll love reading about the gangsters—and they'll learn that trying to mandate social behavior is a slippery slope.

Can I See Your I.D.? True Stories of False Identities, by Chris Barton (2011). We live in a world where someone can rather easily steal our identity. This book relates ten such stories. Developing readers can manage one story at a time rather than facing a whole book at once.

Claudette Colvin: Twice Toward Justice, by Phillip Hoose (2009). We know about Rosa Parks, but this teenager did the very same thing earlier. Learn why we have never heard her name.

The Elephant Scientist, by Caitlin and Donna M. Jackson (Scientists in the Field Series, 2011). An entry in an ideal series for middle schoolers. The books follow scientists as they study a particular animal, work in outer space, or track trash moved by the movement of the ocean. Each story is well told and beautifully illustrated. Kids pore over the photographs and read to find out what is going on behind them.

Flesh and Blood So Cheap: The Triangle Fire and Its Legacy, by Albert Marrin (2011). In the days before unions and standards of safety in factories, the Triangle Shirt Company felt entirely comfortable locking their workers in the factory. When a fire erupted and no one could flee, things had to change.

Frozen Man, by David Getz (1994). When a corpse is found in the snow, the man is identified as being five thousand years old. Yikes! (Written at a second- to third-grade reading level.)

The Good, the Bad, and the Barbie, by Tanya Lee Stone (2010). Barbie is a national icon, and the history of how she became the biggest-selling doll is fascinating. Just seeing her evolution in the photographs is amazing.

Heart and Soul: The Story of America and African Americans, by Kadir Nelson (2011). An examination of the complicated relationship America has had with African Americans and how that almost split the country in two, literally. The art is stunning.

His Name Was Raoul Wallenberg: Courage, Rescue, and Mystery During World War II, by Louis Borden (2012). Written in free verse. Raoul Wallenberg was one of the great resistance fighters during World War II. The inspiring story of one man trying to make a difference.

Hitler Youth: Growing Up in Hitler's Shadow, by Susan Campbell Bartoletti (2005). Bartoletti is a master of making history come to life. In this book we learn about Hitler's idea to inculcate Nazi doctrine in Germany under the guise of a "boy-scout like" organization. We also encounter teens who joined the resistance movement at great risk to their own lives (some died).

How They Croaked: The Awful Ends of the Awfully Famous by Georgia Bragg (2011). Made for dipping into. Your eyes move all over the page from one interesting thing to another. Among the awfully famous are Einstein, Marie Curie, and Blackbeard.

Invincible Microbe: Tuberculosis and the Never-Ending Search for a Cure, by Jim Murphy and Alison Blank (2012). The authors tell such a great story (about something most kids know nothing about) it's hard to believe it's nonfiction. Murphy's book *An American Plague*, which recounts the yellow fever epidemic of 1793, won just about every nonfiction award there is.

Knucklehead: Tall Tales & Mostly True Stories About Growing Up Scieszka, by Jon Scieszka (2008). This autobiography is one of the funniest book kids will ever read.

Life in Prison, by Stanley "Tookie" Williams (1998). Kids are interested in reading about gangs but not necessarily in joining one. But if they ever did want to join one, this cautionary autobiography, by the co-founder of the Crips gang in Los Angeles, will steer them away. It's also short and relatively easy to read.

Lincoln Shot: A President's Life Remembered, by Barry Denenberg, illustrated by Christopher Bing (2008). This oversize book looks like a newspaper from the day Lincoln was shot.

Lincoln Through the Lens: How Photography Revealed and Shaped an Extraordinary Life, by Martin W. Sandler (2008). The Civil War came to life in the battle scene photographs of Mathew Brady. Lincoln was the first president who had to deal with the pros and cons of this emerging technology.

Making Comics: Storytelling Secrets of Comics, Manga and Graphic Novels, by Scott McCloud (2006). An enormously popular book that shows kids how they might create their own comics.

Marching for Freedom: Walk Together, Children, and Don't You Grow Weary, by Elizabeth Partridge (2009). A wonderful book on the freedom marches during the civil rights movement. The photographs are compelling and heartbreaking.

Mr. Lincoln's High-Tech War: How the North Used the Telegraph, Railroads, Surveillance Balloons, Ironclads, High-Powered Weapons, and More to Win the Civil War, by Thomas B. Allen (2009). Another book on Lincoln and the Civil War and the part the new technology played in winning the war.

Purple Death: The Mysterious Flu of 1918, by David Getz (2000). The great flu pandemic of 1918 is mentioned whenever a new strain of flu appears to be taking hold. An easy-to-read account of just how that flu epidemic became as deadly as it was. (Written at a second- to third-grade reading level.)

Secrets of a Civil War Submarine: Solving the Mysteries of the H. L. Hunley, by Sally M. Walker (2005). When the Hunley was discovered, no one knew the stories it would tell.

Temple Grandin: How the Girl Who Loved Cows Embraced Autism and Changed the World, by Sy Montgomery (2012). Temple Grandin used the insights gained from her autism to create better living conditions for cattle. A great look at how seeing things differently can be a good thing.

They Called Themselves the K.K.K.: The Birth of an American Terrorist Group, by Susan Campbell Bartoletti (2010). The history of the first terrorist group in our country and its far reach into our culture.

Witches! The Absolutely True Story of Disaster in Salem, by Rosalyn Schanzer (2011). Explains what happened to the girls "bewitched" in Salem in 1692.

NONFICTION PICTURE BOOKS

Buried Alive! How 33 Miners Survived 69 Days Deep Under the Chilean Desert, by Elaine Scott (2012). The title says it all.

Me . . . Jane, by Patrick McDonnell (2011). A wonderful book about Jane Goodall, whose work with chimpanzees has been groundbreaking.

Meet the Dogs of Bedlam Farm, by Jon Katz (2011). For kids who love dogs. Describes a group of dogs on a farm in upstate New York and all their jobs on the farm.

Saving Audie, by Dorothy Hinshaw Patent, photos by William Muñoz (2011). Ever wonder what happened to those pit bulls rescued from Michael Vick's house? Audie is one of them.

Bodies from the Ash: Life and Death in Ancient Pompeii (2005); *Bodies from the Bog* (2003); and *Bodies from the Ice: Melting Glaciers and the Recovery of the Past* (2008); all by James M. Deem. These books feature eye-catching covers, and the possibility of grossness pulls boy readers in. All three deal with natural ways dead bodies have been preserved. *Bodies from the Ash* describes how the lava preserved some people caught in volcano eruption while going about their daily life in Pompeii. *Bodies from the Bog* talks about bodies remarkably preserved in peat bogs. *Bodies from the Ice* discusses intact bodies frozen for centuries.

Two Bobbies: A True Story of Hurricane Katrina, Friendship, and Survival, by Kirby Larson and Mary Nethery, illustrated by Jean Cassels (2008). A dog who is tied up manages to break free and save himself and a blind cat from the rising waters brought on by Hurricane Katrina in New Orleans.

Wilma Unlimited: How Wilma Rudolph Became the World's Fastest Woman, by Kathleen Krull, illustrated by David Diaz (1996). A fantastic book about a fantastic woman. Wilma Rudolph survived polio and many other limiting factors in her life and went on to become the fastest female runner in the world.

Owen & Mzee: The Language of Friendship, by Isabella Hatkoff, Craig Hatkoff, and Dr. Paula Kahumba (2006). After the tsunami in the Indian Ocean in 2004, a hippopotamus and a giant tortoise form a heretofore unheard-of friendship. Animal lovers love this book.

Team Moon: How 400,000 People Landed Apollo 11 on the Moon, by Catherine Thimmesh (2006). How many people did it take to put men on the moon? You won't believe how many, or the variety of things they did to make this remarkable effort succeed.

A Dozen Books to Grab (Primarily) Boys

The first five titles on this list are described either in this chapter or an earlier one (the specific chapter is included in parentheses).

1. *Stormbreaker*, by Anthony Horowitz (Alex Ryder series) (Chapter 3)
2. *Knucklehead*, by Jon Scieszka (Chapter 1)
3. *The Strange Case of Origami Yoda*, by Tom Angleberger (Chapter 3)
4. Big Nate series, by Lincoln Peirce (Chapter 3)
5. *Yummy*, by G. Neri (graphic novel) (Chapter 3)
6. *Homeboyz*, by Alan Sitomer (2007). When Teddy's little sister is gunned down accidentally in a drive-by shooting, Teddy retaliates but is arrested before anyone is seriously hurt. A mentoring program pairs Teddy with twelve-year-old Micah, who is on the verge of becoming involved in a gang. Will Teddy steer him away from gangs?
7. The NERDS series, by Michael Buckley (various dates). It's not nerds as in *dorks*, it's NERDS as in National Espionage, Rescue, and Defense Society. True, the members are nerds, but they have some amazing abilities that turn them from nerds into NERDS. Think of this series as light-hearted, goofy Alex Ryder stories. They're very funny!
8. *Chasing Lincoln's Killer*, by James Swanson (2009). This very compelling book is written by the author of the *New York Times* bestseller *Manhunt*. Kids will be astounded by how John Wilkes Booth even got into the Ford Theater and how he was able to escape after shooting Lincoln. It's all true and extraordinarily interesting.

9. *Split*, by Swati Avasthi (2010). Jace has finally left home after his father has beaten him up one time too many. He tracks down his older brother, who he hopes can help him build a new life. What weighs on both brothers is that their mother, who is also no stranger to their father's fists, is still home with him.

10. *Middle School, the Worst Years of My Life*, by James Patterson (2011). Patterson moved from his adult thrillers to the middle school market with his entertaining Maximum Ride series. This stand-alone book echoes the Diary of a Wimpy Kid books in format and story. If students like the Wimpy Kid series, they'll like this one too.

11. *Lawn Boy*, by Gary Paulsen (2007). A funny story about a twelve-year-old who starts a lawn-mowing business to make some extra dollars over the summer. A client barters his investment services for getting his lawn cut, and before you know it, Lawn Boy is rolling in money. If the book weren't so funny it could be an economics lesson!

12. *Rucker Park Setup*, by Paul Volponi (2007). Anyone interested in basketball won't be able to put it down. Two buddies, J.R. and Mackey, are constant fixtures on the neighborhood court in Harlem until the day J.R. is stabbed to death. Mackey, who feels somewhat responsible, is determined to settle the score on the court and on the streets. Like any mystery, this story keeps you on the edge of your seat until the end.

A Dozen Books to Grab (Primarily) Girls

1. *Mockingbird*, by Kathryn Erskine (2011). Caitlin suffers from Asperger's syndrome and has difficulty knowing how to act in a lot of situations. Her brother, Devon, used to help her when she needed it. Now Devon is dead and she is left to cope on her own. She is also dealing with the grief of losing her brother. Caitlin ultimately helps her father manage his grief as well.

2. *Savvy*, by Ingrid Law (2010). When each child in the Beaumont family turns thirteen, their savvy—a magical ability—is revealed to them. Mibs is really hoping hers is something that can help her dad, who has been in an auto accident. On the way to visit him in the hospital, Mibs and her siblings unleash their savvies in some astounding ways.

3. *Num8ers*, by Rachel Ward (2010). This is a real page-turner! Jem has a unique ability to see numbers when she sees a person. She has no idea what the numbers mean until the day she and her boyfriend, Spider, are at the London Eye. She sees all the people lined up to ride the Eye and she is stunned to see the same number for each person—today's date. She and Spider take off running and moments later the Eye explodes. Why does Jem see these numbers and what will it do to her now that she

knows what the numbers mean? In the meantime, the police are looking for two teens who were seen running from the Eye moments before the explosion.

4. *Shiver*, by Maggie Stiefvater (2009). This book satisfies the supernatural cravings of those who have charged through the Twilight series. Grace lives on the edge of the woods and has always been drawn to the wolves she sees there. Sam is a boy she knows who works in the local bookstore for a few months each year. When the two meet, they sense a deep connection. Sam is a shape shifter—human in the warm weather, a wolf in the true cold. It's a girl-meets-boy/wolf story you keep reading to find out whether Grace and Sam are able to stay together. (The series continues in two other books, *Linger* and *Forever*.)

5. *The Sixty-Eight Rooms*, by Marianne Malone (2010). In the Chicago Art Institute there is a gallery of miniature rooms, each from a different era in history, crafted by Mrs. James Ward Thorne in the 1930s. Ruthie and a friend find a key that allows them to shrink and go inside these rooms. Will they be able to return to normal size? Although the book is not illustrated, readers can go online and see the miniature rooms in which the story is set. (There is a sequel titled *Stealing Magic*.)

6. *Love, Aubrey*, by Suzanne LaFleur (2009). Aubrey and her mother survived the accident that took her father and her younger sister. Her mother, devastated by grief, leaves one day and doesn't return. Aged eleven, Aubrey can manage for a bit on her own but soon begins to worry about food and other essentials. Then her grandmother appears and takes her to Vermont. While she is well cared for and certainly loved by her grandmother, how does an abandoned child ever learn to trust and to love again?

7. *Touch Blue*, by Cynthia Lord (2010). Tess lives on a small island off the coast of Maine that bustles with people and activity during the summer. However, when the summer folks leave, the town shrinks down to a small, close-knit community. So small, in fact, that the state of Maine decides to shut down the school on the island because there are so few students. This may mean that the few remaining families will have to leave the island. In an effort to increase enrollment, the community brings in foster children, and one of those kids, Aaron, moves in with Tess's family. Tess grows to love Aaron like a brother, and when problems arise, she wants him to be okay more than anything. But will he be?

8. *Emma-Jean Lazarus Fell in Love*, by Lauren Tarshis (2009). Emma-Jean is a quirky and very smart young girl who never really fits in. She doesn't "get" her classmates, and they don't "get" her. When she sees Colleen crying in the bathroom, Emma-Jean decides to use her smarts to think through Colleen's problem with her keen analytical mind. But sometimes the

problems middle school girls face are not best solved by analyzing them. Emma-Jean is in way over her head!

9. *Wintergirls*, by Laurie Halse Anderson (2009). This powerful book about anorexia is for sophisticated readers who like slightly edgy books. Lia and Cassie are best friends and, unfortunately, partners in trying to become the thinnest girls they know. Anorexia is nothing to fool around with and, sadly, Cassie goes too far and dies from complications related to the disease. This story gets inside the head of Lia as she hits bottom with her anorexia and begins to see that there may be more to life than starving herself.

10. *Flyaway*, by Lucy Christopher (2011). Isla and her father have a tradition of going out to the lake when the geese arrive to winter there. On this particular visit, the unfortunate geese fly into a new power line and some are killed. One in particular has gotten separated from its flock. Isla's father collapses at the lake and is rushed to the hospital, and Isla's world turns upside down. As she tries to put everything in perspective, she meets Harry, who is in the same hospital, suffering from leukemia. She and Harry come up with an idea about how to get the lone goose able to fly back to its flock. In her mind, Isla believes that if the goose can accomplish this, Harry and her dad will recover as well.

11. *Camo Girl*, by Kekla Magoon (2011). Ella is a biracial child who is teased for her mottled skin tones. She feels like an outsider in her middle school, partly because she sticks by her old friend, Z (who is a really weird kid), because it's the right thing to do. When Bailey arrives at school and is instantly popular, she is astonished that he wants to hang with her. But if Bailey doesn't want to hang around with Z, what will Ella do?

12. *Pie*, by Sarah Weeks (2011). Alice lives in a small town and is very close to her Aunt Polly, who makes the best pies in the world. Her pie shop is busy all the time. When Aunt Polly dies rather suddenly, everyone wants her recipes. No one knows to whom she left the recipes, and all kinds of jealousies and fights begin. As it turns out, Aunt Polly left the recipes to her awful cat, Lardo—and Lardo is in Alice's care. Now what does she do?

LAST WORDS

Being aware of possible biases helps ensure that our classrooms and libraries are well stocked with titles that will grab boys and titles that will grab girls—and that will encourage crossover. Bottom line: there should be loads of books available so that students feel free to choose what suits them best. Meeting kids where they are always pays off.

Then, too, not every child is going to become an avid reader, and we have to admit that people can live full lives without being one. It's taken me a long time to be able to say that, because I read constantly and can't imagine my life without it. But not everyone is like me. If we accept alternate formats as reading, our kids will begin to see reading as useful and interesting. This just might open up other areas of reading to them as well.

The biggest thing to remember is that all the students in your class are individuals who will gravitate to what they want to read. Kids surprise us on a daily basis. Those surprises and our successes with individual students make working with them the joy it is.

Setting the Stage

HARNESSING THE POWER OF READERS' RESPONSES IN DISCUSSION

Paul Volponi's edgy books grab kids from the first sentence, and he never lets them go until the end of the book. His novels are contemporary and fast paced, and the urgency in his prose pulls readers in from the start. When an author manages to make connections with kids the way Volponi does, we, as teachers, must be sensitive to what we do to his books in the name of teaching literature. We have to figure out a way to preserve the reader's experience with this kind of authentic literature and still come up with a grade. I think it can be done.

FEATURED AUTHOR: **Paul Volponi**

When I sit down to write for a young adult audience, I look for themes and situations that have touched me deeply. I want the reader to feel my emotions, and to share them. Of course, I don't want to tell readers exactly how to feel, or what to think. Ultimately, that's for the reader to decide. I just want to share. I want to hold a mirror up to society and show an accurate reflection. I want a novel to start out running, not walking. I'm willing to put flesh on the bones of my characters as we move along. It's one of the reasons that I think my novels are seen by educators as highly discussable for a classroom full of students—because I don't shy away from difficult topics like racism, inequality, and the sometimes blurry line between right and wrong. I give students something to talk about by presenting multiple sides of problems that don't have easy answers. I believe that my novels inspire teens to think differently about the way they conduct themselves, and the way they perceive others' actions.

I want to grab the reader's attention from the start and not let go. I don't like downtime in the plots, or action that lags behind the narrative. I want it all to run simultaneously, so you can't afford to let your guard down for a single sentence.

I write books for teens in the first person because I believe it binds students to the protagonist, allowing the reader to feel his every breath. I write from real life, often using experiences I've had or things that I've witnessed on basketball courts, at schools in drug rehab centers, and on Rikers Island in New York City, the world's largest jail.

I'm driven to write for teens because they are the ultimate underdogs. They have the exact same problems as adults and much less power to solve them. And they have too often heard from adults that their problems are trivial. I want their problems to be the most important things in the world in my novels. Hopefully, I create a jumping-off place for them to discuss, and even resolve, these situations.

I hope our teens keep reading and striving for more. As a YA author, I feel like I can help them along. And the boundless reach of a library shelf or a school bookroom allows me to speak to teens I've never even met.

Chapter Four

WHY ON EARTH DID I ASK THAT?

Prompting Productive Discussions

uestioning is a key part of being a teacher. We construct quizzes on the books students have supposedly read in order to verify whether they did indeed read them and have understood what they read. But questioning is far more complicated than that. How we question, why we question, and what we learn from our questioning all need to be considered. In the name of assessment, we often give kids tests that don't meet our objectives.

CAN WE "TEACH" BOOKS?

I often hear teachers talking with one another about teaching a book: "I teach *Bud, Not Buddy* in my class. Do you?" It seems a strange thing to say. What do they mean? How do you teach a book? Earlier I mentioned that my son's experience with Susan Cooper's *The Dark Is Rising* came down to a list of ludicrous assignments meant to supply his teacher with grades. None of the assignments did anything to enhance and extend his understanding of the book. This is how some teachers "teach" a book.

On the other hand, there are teachers who do great things when they share a book with their students. Laura Robb, an extraordinary teacher, met the author Katherine Paterson many years ago and confided that she used Paterson's *Bridge to Terabithia* (1977) in her classroom. Paterson cringed inside at Robb's words, because she remembered all the books that had been ruined for her when she was in school. Later, fearing the worst, Paterson sat in the back of Robb's classroom, an anonymous visitor, as Robb and her students discussed the book. But at the end of that day, an elated Paterson told Robb she was welcome to use her book anytime in any classroom anywhere. Paterson had encountered a teacher who did not hand out worksheets with questions like "What color does Leslie's father paint the living room?" (The correct answer to that, by the way, is "Who cares!") Instead, these kids grappled with the idea of loss so beautifully described in the book.

Recently I had the opportunity to hear Paterson speak. After her remarks, a woman in the audience asked whether having a character in the book die might be too much for a fifth grader to deal with. Paterson responded (with an eloquence I can only paraphrase) that the death of someone close to us is something all human beings experience, some later in life, but some quite early. Reading about such a loss allows children a trial run at the experience without the burden of it actually happening. Sharing books in a deep and meaningful way allows kids to think about and understand what they are reading.

We do not teach books—we share them. We select a particular book for a reason: not any book will do. It's not the book we teach but the theme. If we are teaching a unit on justice, we select books that have justice at their core. One might be *Shiloh*, by Phyllis Reynolds Naylor (1991), which centers around who owns—and who deserves to own—the eponymous dog. Wouldn't it be just if Marty got to keep him? Another might be *Monster*, by Walter Dean Myers (1999), a much more serious book about right versus wrong and the shades of gray in between. Is it just for Stephen to be given the same punishment the shooters receive?

The book is the vehicle for our teaching. I say that with some reluctance, because I think of books as high art and referring to them as vehicles makes me wince. You get the point, though. We turn kids on to books that are springboards for discussion and help them see what they may have missed in a superficial reading. Encountering characters who are dealing with unjust situations helps students begin to understand what justice is. That's teaching!

Do all books merit discussion? No. Sometimes we just want to read a book for fun—our "Twinkie reads," a term I encountered in a *Washington Post* editorial some years ago. The writer (unfortunately, I no longer remember his or her name) mentioned that we all know we should eat from the five food groups but every once in a while we sneak in a Twinkie. The same goes for reading. We know we should read good literature but every now and then we read something light and silly just for the fun of it. Reading for pure enjoyment is one of the great reasons for wanting to read.

QUESTIONING GONE WRONG

We need to reexamine how we use questioning in our classrooms. Sadly, many teachers, rather than talking about the book's characters and themes and discovering kids' reactions, rely on quizzes to find out whether students have read the books they've been assigned. If we want to kill a book, this is a big first step toward achieving our goal. If a book is worth reading in a deep and meaningful way (and why would we ask our students to read one that isn't?), it deserves more than becoming the basis for ten low-level questions. (Also, I hate to tell you this, but students can easily pass the quiz without doing the assigned reading, and vice versa.)

READER PROFILE ▶ Color It Pointless

When my son was in the third grade he had to read *Little House on the Prairie*—and to my surprise, he didn't hate it. He did hate the ten questions he had to answer after nearly every chapter. One evening he expressed his frustration about "these stupid questions." I decided to read the chapter and try my hand at the questions. There were some I couldn't answer either, one of them being, "What color were Pa's suspenders?" Who cares! Do you think Laura Ingalls Wilder wants us to remember forever that bit of information, intended to help us see the character in our mind's eye? Good readers read to get the main idea, the gist of the story. We do not retain every factoid, every bit of minutiae. Like computers, our brains are only so big and can store only a certain amount of data. We discard things like the color of a character's suspenders because we recognize it as an unimportant detail. We don't need to remember it.

Teachers often complain that their kids don't get the main idea when they read. That may well be true, but I think we sometimes create the problem by pointing them in the wrong direction. If they know we are going to be asking detail-oriented questions rather than ones having to do with the theme of the book, they become disinterested. If we keep asking kids to focus on the minutiae, how will they ever get around to noticing the larger message? We send students the wrong message every time we ask them an unimportant question in the name of finding out whether they read the material. It's quite possible for children to fail such quizzes, especially if they've read the assignment with an eye on the big picture. Imagine receiving a failing grade for doing what they were supposed to do, for being ready to discuss what happened in the book. Where is the sense in that?

In a survey I conducted at Warren County Middle School, one of the students voiced his opinion that *"Tuck Everlasting* sucks eggs!" His emphatic statement shocked me. Like *Bridge to Terabithia*, *Tuck Everlasting* (1975) is a brilliant piece of writing, and it brings up the issue of immortality. Would you really like to live forever? This boy had clearly not read and discussed the book but simply answered inane questions about it. In fact, I have the quiz and one of the questions is, "What color suit does the stranger wear?" Honestly, first the color of Pa's suspenders, now the suit color of the stranger's suit. What is it with this color fixation that turns up in quizzes! If I were asked such inconsequential questions each time I read a book, I think I would develop the same attitude. We turn kids off to books with quizzes like these, and no teacher wants that to happen.

This is why I do not use—nor approve of—Accelerated Reader and similar computer programs. Computers cannot score open-ended responses. They score yes-and-no questions and ones that are clearly right or wrong—the very questions that do not support real learning and discussion. No discussion is prompted by a question like "What color were Pa's suspenders?" You either name the right color or you don't; there's nothing to talk about. Some teachers say they like Accelerated Reader because it motivates their kids to read. It doesn't. It motivates them to pass the test and amass points that can then be traded in for a reward. Mallette, Henk, and Melnick (2004) have shown that programs like this do not foster long-term motivation. They do not turn kids into lifelong readers. Engaging students in discussions that intrigue them makes them want to return to books for more of the same.

Not long ago I received a thank-you note from the daughter of a former student for some books I'd sent. After expressing her gratitude, the girl bemoaned the fact that, unfortunately, they were not Accelerated Reader books, so she wouldn't be able to read them. Her mother let the daughter send the note instead of balling it up and throwing it in the trash, because she too believes that Accelerated Reader is not about comprehension, and she wanted me to be aware of another drawback to the program. Kids who participate in Accelerated Reader choose books that have quizzes over ones that don't—a huge limitation. They also choose books based on the number of points they can get for reading them. The purpose of reading is overridden by the desire to win a game and get a prize. What message is that sending?

Another troubling aspect of these tests that is that they force kids to be convergent thinkers—they don't see the options beyond a yes-or-no answer. Divergent thinkers see possibilities everywhere and want to explore where these possibilities may take them. The complicated, technological world we live in will have far more use for divergent thinkers who can see all sides of a problem than it will for convergent thinkers who cannot. Ultimately, comprehension is not about right and wrong but about teasing meaning from the facts before us.

Every teacher at one time or other has fallen into the trap of using ten-question quizzes. I know I did. We're busy, and using the same test again and again makes the load a little lighter. And we're checking their comprehension, right? Look at a quiz you once used. What kinds of questions does it contain? Do they require right or wrong answers or invite real thinking? Are the answers to the questions found directly in the piece your students read or do they require some synthesizing of the material? By taking an honest look at our practice, we see where change needs to occur.

QUESTIONS THAT MATTER

To use questioning effectively, we need to move from questions that require no higher-order thinking to ones that require students to infer and synthesize information. Taffy Raphael developed a way of looking at questioning that helped me realize how important questioning is and how asking unimportant questions does students a disservice. She developed her question-answer-relationship strategy, or QAR, in 1982, and it remains an important way to help teachers move away from low-level questions toward questions that foster discussion and get at what is important in a given piece.

Raphael identifies four kinds of questions that are routinely used. The first two, "right there" and "think and search," are fairly literal, "in the book" questions whose answers can be found by going back to the text.

A right-there question about *Freedom Summer*, by Deborah Wiles (2011), would be, "What is the main character's name?" The protagonist's name is Joe. (I had to look that up in my copy, because I couldn't remember it. And I didn't remember it because it's unimportant in the story.)

A think-and-search question about the same book is, "What kinds of things do the boys do together?" They swim in the creek, pester John Henry's grandmother, and run around in the heat. A think-and-search question is more advanced than a right-there question, because we have to search the text for the things the boys did. It is not quite the no-brainer a right-there question is, because it asks the reader to think relationally. For example, if I ask students who are reading *Martin's Big Words: The Life of Dr. Martin Luther King, Jr.*, by Doreen Rappaport (2001), to look for some of the things Dr. King accomplished during his lifetime, the list would reveal how great a leader he was. Think-and-search questions often produce a fairly rote re-counting of facts, but in the hands of a good teacher, those facts can lead to a revealing discussion.

The remaining two kinds of questions, "author and me" and "on my own," are the direct opposite of rote. They are engaging and make readers think critically. Raphael refers to them as "in my head" questions: we have to use our head to answer them!

An author-and-me question asks readers to take what they learned in the story and connect it to their own experience. An author-and-me question about *Freedom Summer* might be, "Why do you think John Henry wanted to pay for his own ice pop at the end of the story?" Students have to think about what has happened to John Henry that caused him to assert himself and about how they might feel in his shoes. There can be and often are several good answers to a question like this. By demanding to buy his own ice pop, John Henry, who is the victim of racial injustice, is taking charge of the world in a tangible way. He is also buying the ice pop in order to enter the store where up to now he has been unwelcome. There are any number of insights into John Henry's action, and if we open the door to sharing them, kids see that (within limits) there isn't a right or wrong answer and that they can turn to their peers for good ideas.

The last kind of question, on-my-own, is the most useful. Students do not have to have read the book to answer it. The answer comes from what they know of the world and what they think. An on-my-own question about *Freedom Summer* might be whether or not laws change attitudes. Because you do not have to have read the book to answer an on-my-own question, it's a good one to use when introducing a book. The question gets the students thinking about why the book is important.

In the case of *Freedom Summer*, my students are initially on both sides of the fence before reading. Most say laws don't change attitudes, but there is always one who amends the statement to "Can laws change atti-tudes over time?" Therein lies the discussion. When there are several good ideas on the table, I turn the kids loose on the book with those ideas in mind. When they have finished reading it, we revisit the question in light of what they've read. Imagine the discussion this setup enables: kids think out loud, bounce ideas off one another, and work collaboratively to understand the realities of the civil rights movement. What's more im-portant? That they know the main character is named Joe or that they now have a new understanding about civil issues and personal conduct and responsibility?

Identifying the kinds of questions being asked helps students do well on standardized tests. Those tests typically ask low-level right-there and think-and-search questions. Just as the answers to those questions can be found by looking back in the book, they can be answered by revisiting the test passage. Letting the students in on the "secret" of how questions are created gives them a leg up when it comes to answering those questions on a high-stakes test. And knowing that we think they can handle the heavier, deeper questions gives them much more confidence in their abilities.

FOSTERING DISCUSSION WITH READ-ALOUDS

Books should be read aloud in every classroom. By that I mean that at least once a day the teacher should grab a book, let the kids get comfortable, and read aloud to them. It can be a picture book shared in one session, it can be a chapter book completed over a series of days, it can be fiction or nonfiction, it can be anything the kids find engaging. Kids love to be read to, even in middle school. A fabulous book to read aloud is the 2012 Newbery winner, *Dead End in Norvelt*, by Jack Gantos (2011). Part humor, part pathos, the book is so entertaining that kids will beg for more each time you stop.

Reading aloud is a wonderful teaching tool because it fulfills so many needs in a language arts classroom. Sitting and listening together helps create a social, literate classroom community. As the teacher, you are sending a strong message that reading is so important that you are spending valuable class time doing it.

Reading books aloud to your class effectively levels the playing field. Not all your students are reading at the same level, so reading aloud lets all the kids experience a book and take part in the discussion. It is a shared, literate experience kids really enjoy.

Reading aloud also reinforces a "sense of story." Kids who haven't read a lot of stories often don't understand how stories work—that they have a beginning, middle, and end and that there is generally a problem that is resolved—and are therefore more likely to have comprehension problems. If we don't understand how something works, it is harder to make sense of it. Exposing kids to more and more stories and mapping out one or two boosts their comprehension.

Another huge benefit of reading aloud is that it increases students' vocabulary. It makes sense: stopping as you are reading aloud to point out a fabulous word shows students that words are interesting. Asking them to provide some synonyms for that fabulous word afterward is fun too. Kids who read have far better vocabularies than kids who don't.

Reading aloud is especially useful as a motivator: it allows kids to hear how fluent reading sounds, it gives them access to a book they might not otherwise have been able to read with ease, and it shows them that books are important and relevant. Every kid can participate, because reading level doesn't matter.

One of the best things about reading is that it lets us travel anywhere, walk in the shoes of characters whose lives are very different from our own, and acquire information on just about anything that piques our interest. Reading aloud lets these things happen for everyone in the class at the same time. When I heard Jim Trelease, author of *The Read-Aloud Handbook*, speak, he noted that reading aloud conditions the brain to associate reading with pleasure. If the kids in our class are all truly caught up in the book we are reading aloud, they will develop positive associations with reading that carry over to reading on their own.

Reading aloud is also a great way to introduce kids to a variety of genres. It shows children what the world of books can offer them. Children who have not been read to regularly or have stayed away from books because they aren't very good at reading often don't realize what awaits them in books. Who would have thought that there were autobiographies like *Knucklehead*, by Jon Scieszka (2008), that will have them laughing out loud? Or that a nonfiction book like *Dr. Jenner and the Speckled Monster: The Search for the Smallpox Vaccine*, by Albert Marrin (2002), could read like a detective novel? Or that a boy named Harry Potter could lead such an interesting life? Reading is way cool!

With all of these incredible reasons for reading aloud to our classes, why wouldn't we? Nevertheless, I hear teachers say they can't "waste" time like that and still cover the state standards. That's being penny-wise and pound foolish. Reading aloud is one of the best ways to ensure that your kids meet the language arts standards. It is anything but a waste of time.

READING PICTURE BOOKS ALOUD TO MODEL DISCUSSION

Appendix B is an extensive list of picture books suitable for older readers. Reading one of these books aloud at the start of a unit can pique students' interest and head them in the direction we want them to go. It jumpstarts a collaborative discussion and makes their subsequent reading on the topic or theme that much richer. For example, an interesting book to read to open a unit on World War II for older kids is *Faithful Elephants: A True Story of Animals, People and War*, by Yukio Tsuchiya (1988). It is a wonderfully written, true account of the animals in the Tokyo zoo during World War II, who were destroyed because the authorities were afraid an errant bomb might hit the zoo and the animals would escape, wreaking havoc wherever they went.

I generally begin by asking, "What does it mean when people talk about the cost of war?" Some students take the question literally and mention the huge dollar cost of the wars in Iraq and Afghanistan. Others talk about the human cost and how soldiers die in wars. I tell them that both answers are important and that to me the most significant cost of war is the loss of human life. Then I say that this book will introduce them to still another cost of war.

I then read *Faithful Elephants* (with a box of tissues at the ready). The Tokyo zookeepers ultimately feel that the danger of having animals roaming the street is too high and decide to kill them. The story zeroes in on three elephants, who go from performing tricks before crowds for treats to being starved to death. This book always evokes a very visceral reaction; no one condones animal abuse. Kids burst with questions: "Why didn't they just move them to a safer place?" "Why did they starve them? That's cruel. Why not shoot them?"

But do they realize that these and worse things happen to humans in wars? This question is a natural segue to a conversation about how humans were treated during the Holocaust. How is it that we cry for the animals but not as readily for the victims of the Nazis? Is it because the animals are perceived as innocent creatures entrusted to our care? Students always come to the realization that Hitler's victims were innocent as well and deserving of our concern. One short picture book, so much worth discussing.

A SAMPLING OF PICTURE BOOKS FOR OLDER READERS

Here are a few titles I love to use with older kids because they generate such wonderful discussions. Not only do they lay the groundwork for a meaningful discussion, but the students get to hear oral language at its best.

1. *The Day Gogo Went to Vote*, by Elinor Batezat Sisulu, illustrated by Sharon Wilson (1996). Blacks finally win the right to vote in 1994 in South Africa and Gogo (Great-Grandmother) is determined to cast her vote.

2. *The Mysteries of Harris Burdick*, by Chris Van Allsburg (1984). Fourteen strange and thought-provoking pictures and captions invite readers to make up their own story.

3. *The Stranger*, by Chris Van Allsburg (1986). A farmer hits something in the road and is surprised to find a man, not a deer, lying there. But who is this man who doesn't talk, is dressed in leather clothes, and is able to pick up rabbits and stroke them?

4. *The Sweetest Fig*, by Chris Van Allsburg (1993). Monsieur Bibot, a French dentist, is given two supposedly magical figs (they can make dreams come true) as payment for some dentistry. Bibot eats one before going to bed and has a dream that comes true. Then, to make sure the remaining fig is not wasted, he learns to control his dreams. This is a superb introduction to characterization. It is also the basis for a fun writing prompt: What if you had the chance to make your wildest dreams come true?

5. *The Widow's Broom*, by Chris Van Allsburg (1992). When a strange broom is found in the widow's house, the neighbors are fearful. How do people react when they are afraid? What might the broom represent?

6. *Rose Blanche*, by Roberto Innocenti (1985). A young girl in Nazi-occupied Europe discovers children held prisoner in a nearby concentration camp and brings them food. The implication that the girl dies makes this an interesting book to talk about.

7. *Science Verse*, by Jon Scieszka, illustrated by Lane Smith (2004). This is parody at its best, hilarious science poetry modeled after some well-known poems such as "Casey at the Bat," by Ernest Thayer.

8. *The True Story of the 3 Little Pigs!*, by Jon Scieszka, illustrated by Lane Smith (1989). What if the Big Bad Wolf was only setting out to get a cup of sugar for a cake for his dear old granny? This book has it all: point of view, persuasive writing, and parody.

9. *Terrible Things*, by Eve Bunting, illustrated by Stephen Gammell (1980). A small white rabbit asks his father why the Terrible Things keep coming to take away animals in their small community. The big rabbit says he should be glad that it isn't them. This is a great introduction to the Holocaust via allegory.

TRY IT OUT
A Word About Minilessons

Wide reading and discussion alone do not guarantee that our students will become eager, lifelong readers; direct instruction has to be part of the reading workshop as well. This is what teachers find hardest to grapple with: How do we fit instruction into this paradigm? I asked the WCMS teachers to read Laura Robb's book *Teaching Reading in Middle School* (2000), so we could see how a master teacher balances direct instruction with lots of reading.

We talked about the idea of the minilesson—a short bit of instruction (generally ten or fifteen minutes) on a concept that needs to be covered or an issue that has arisen—and how it fits into the reading workshop. For example, if our students are having a tough time identifying themes, we might think aloud as we identify the theme of a picture book in a minilesson, so they'll see how an experienced reader does this. It will probably take more than one minilesson to bring kids where we want them to be, and revisiting an issue several days later is fine. Spending an entire class period going over and over the same material, however, turns students off—and greatly reduces the time they spend reading.

Although minilessons are outside the scope of this book, the WCMS teachers and I found that many of Virginia's language arts Standards of Learning (SOLs) could be met through a combination of wide reading and minilessons, and the same is likely true for most other states. We cannot walk away from teaching vocabulary, the elements of story, and devices like foreshadowing and point of view. Mini-lessons are a perfect way to demonstrate and name these concepts.

WANT TO KNOW WHAT'S ON YOUR STUDENTS' MINDS? ASK THEM!

Talking about books with kids is great fun, because they will tell you what they really think. But a discussion without any parameters leads to silly comments meant to gain attention and in the end is unproductive. With the help of a few "rules," kids can amaze us with what they have to say.

Discussion can be scary for us as teachers if we feel we are working without a net. How do we manage the talk? How do we redirect? What if no one is talking? Discussion is an art and takes some practice before we feel comfortable with it. I like to make up a list of ideas that strike me as I read so that I always have something I can add to the discussion if it slows down or gets off track. As for the discussion itself, how do we manage it?

During the first weeks of school, it's a good idea to brainstorm guidelines for how to have a civilized discussion. Because students are more invested in rules if they have a hand in creating them, it helps to ask them to come up with some ideas for what a productive discussion might look like. Since we won't be controlling their discussions, we shouldn't control (but gently guide) them as they generate rules.

Here are some kinds of behavior students often suggest:

- Listen to one another.
- Don't interrupt.
- Raise your hand if you have something to say.
- Don't put anyone down.
- Stay on track.

After they've had a go, I throw in some additional ideas for them to consider. How about making positive comments first before we get to negative ones?

What about staying away from summaries and sharing personal stories we were reminded of when reading? Most important, I make sure the students get the message that there is no one right answer. When we move away from that construct, a lot more learning will take place during classroom discussions.

Another strategy that helps prepare students for a discussion is having them free write before they start—giving them three minutes to write down any thoughts they have about the book. (Displaying a poster in the room listing things to write about—plot, characters, the main issue or theme of the book, writer's style, genre, etc.—is helpful.) The free write doesn't need to be in complete sentences—it can be a series of phrases or a bulleted list. The important thing is just getting ideas down on paper. Once the three minutes are up, every student should have a few ideas in front of her or him. When you ask students for comments, they'll be ready to participate and no one will be embarrassed.

LAST WORDS

When did we stop asking kids what they think of a book and instead resort to easy-to-score questions with right or wrong answers? Whenever it was, we took a turn down the wrong path and it's time we found the right one again. Answering recall questions undermines students' motivation to continue reading. Discussion, on the other hand, broadens their understanding of the texts they are reading and allows them to make connections with the text that will never be triggered by a ten-question quiz. None of us want to turn any child off to reading. Let's find new ways to share books with students and new ways to evaluate their responses. It is time for change. Death to the ten-question quiz!

THROWING A LIFELINE TO
STRUGGLING READERS

For most of you reading this book, reading is a pleasure. But, as we all know, reading is not fun for some of the kids in our classrooms. They live in fear that they'll be called out on their weak reading abilities in front of all their friends. That fear turns into "attitude," and they make it very clear that they hate reading and they're going to do everything they can to avoid it. It's a coping mechanism so that they don't look like fools. Our classrooms are not set up to help these kids. We assign them readings in textbooks they can't possibly read, and the books they are supposed to read are "classics" like *Treasure Island*. The story is irrelevant to them and the text is too difficult—why would they even bother to try their hand at it?

Jeff Kinney changed reading for a lot of developing readers. For many kids who didn't consider themselves readers, the Diary of a Wimpy Kid books have been the first titles that seem completely relevant and readable. As a result, these kids who were struggling readers have become interested in reading. Maybe the Diary of a Wimpy Kid series is so spot on because Kinney understands these kids more than we knew.

FEATURED AUTHOR: Jeff Kinney

"I wrote a few children's books. Not on purpose."
　　　　　　—STEVEN WRIGHT

Aspiring authors sometimes ask me how to connect with kids through writing. My feeling is that you should be honest with them and tell them stories they can relate to rather than push a grown-up agenda. (And if you throw in a bunch of cartoon drawings, it can't hurt.)

But I never set out to become a children's author, or any kind of author, for that matter. I had my sights set on the funny pages. After the requisite years of rejection letters from the comic syndicates, though, I came to terms with the fact that my cartoon drawings weren't professional grade.

My breakthrough moment came when I realized that if I could only draw at a seventh-grade level, then I should make people think I was doing it on purpose. And so, in January of 1998, I hatched the idea of *Diary of a Wimpy Kid*, the cartoon-laced journal of a middle school boy named Greg Heffley.

I took my time with it. I realized this would be my opus, for better or for worse, and that if I was going to get another series of rejection letters, I wanted to put them off for as long as possible. So I spent the better part of the next decade amassing thousands of pages worth of gags, storylines, and drawings.

Never once in that time did I think I was writing for kids. It's true that I was writing *about* kids, but I felt that I was writing a nostalgia piece. My aim was to make an adult remember what it was like to live in their seventh-grade skin.

When I felt like I was ready, I shared a few samples pages with a publishing house in New York. I pitched the book as a massive 700- to 1,000-page tome aimed at grown-ups. But the publisher gently informed me that what I had actually written was a children's series.

The idea seemed audacious to me at the time. But then I realized I didn't have to change a word to make my stories appropriate for kids (my sensibilities are pretty G-rated anyway). Still, it was mind-blowing to think that, for eight years, I had the completely wrong target audience in mind.

My first book was released in 2007, and, thankfully, kids embraced it. I started getting hundreds of letters a week from parents and teachers, and in almost every one, the same curious phrase was used . . . "reluctant reader." "Thank you for writing a book my reluctant reader enjoys." "This is the first book my reluctant reader has read without being asked."

At first, I thought it was some kind of miracle of probability that so many people were using this same exact phrase. I had never heard those words used together before, and didn't know about the reluctant reader phenomenon. I've since come to understand that "reluctant reader" is indeed an epidemic and the term is, generally speaking, educator-speak for a simpler category: "boys."

Now that I know I'm writing for kids, and for reluctant readers in particular, I'm having fun with it. In a recent *Diary of a Wimpy Kid* book, Greg's mother starts a "Reading is Fun" club for the neighborhood boys. The boys bring in their reading selections, which include video game cheat guides, Sudoku puzzle books, and a pop-up book about sharks. Greg's mom counters with her ideas of "legitimate" reading: *Little Women*, *Old Yeller*, and *The Yearling*. Greg wonders if, for a book to be considered a "classic," a person or an animal has to die at the end (and so do I).

Growing up, my classics were books like *Tales of a Fourth Grade Nothing*, *Freckle Juice*, and the *Ramona Quimby* series. I could see myself in the characters created by Judy Blume and Beverly Cleary, who had a talent for writing about people you felt like you knew because they were a lot like you.

Every so often, someone will complain that Greg Heffley is a flawed protagonist, and I couldn't agree more. In fact, most of the humor in my books comes from Greg's imperfections and flawed point of view. But I think Greg's rough spots are what make him authentic. As a kid, Greg's not yet a fully formed human being. His life is just being documented at an awkward time.

Now that my books have been successful, I marvel at my own failure to see that my work belonged in the children's aisle of bookstores. But I'm grateful for that blindness, because had I known I was writing for kids, my approach would have been completely different.

These days, I still write for that imaginary adult who's surfing the humor aisle at the bookstore. I try to keep the true end-reader, the kid, out of my mind, because the temptation is to impart some sort of lesson. But the reason I think kids have taken to my books is because they're fairly lesson-free. It seems that kids, like adults, read fiction for entertainment.

Chapter Five

HELPING DEVELOPING READERS MOVE FORWARD

ou know those worst-case nightmares we sometimes have before a big exam or a job interview? Consider this one. You check your mailbox in the front office on your way to your classroom to start the day. There, along with a passel of other things that need attention, you find a manual on a new schoolwide plan to deal with armed intruders should they ever enter the building. In the few minutes you have before your students come bursting in, you flip through the document—but it's written in French and is essentially incomprehensible. You can figure out a word like *dangereux* because it looks like *dangerous*, but you can't cobble together any real meaning. Worst of all, there's a sticky note on the cover from your principal in clear English: *Have this read for the faculty meeting this afternoon where we will discuss it in detail*. You know you want to read it, you are required to read it, but you can't make any sense of it.

For a substantial number of students in our classes, this nightmare is all too real. They come to school every day hoping against hope that they will simply survive the day without being singled out or embarrassed by their inability to read. They can read but not as well as the other kids in the classroom, and they are convinced they must be stupid. These kids have somehow been passed along from grade to grade without ever getting the help they need to become decent readers. When they look at a page, it might as well be in a foreign language; they recognize some of the words but never enough to understand what they are reading.

When a sixth grader enters the classroom in September, she or he is issued science, math, and English textbooks written at a sixth-grade level. Whether the child is reading at a sixth-grade level makes no difference. The assumption is that all sixth graders read at a sixth-grade level. Any teacher knows that homogenous classes in which all the students are reading at the same level simply don't exist, except in rare, controlled cases. The average sixth-grade classroom includes a range of reading levels from second grade to high school. Why would we issue these students a one-size-fits-all text? There is no one-size-fits-all anything in life: not in clothing and not in reading level. When we stick our heads in the sand and pretend that all our kids can read that sixth-grade textbook, we set far too many students up for failure—yet somehow we are surprised when students fail.

Dick Allington, a noted reading researcher, hit the nail squarely on the head when he titled a 2002 article "You Can't Learn Much from Books You Can't Read." No one would argue with this seemingly simple premise, but still we persist in giving struggling readers unreadable texts, and they remain below grade level and indifferent to reading. Unless, of course, we decide to meet them where they are and help them begin to move forward. And isn't that our job?

Donalyn Miller, in *The Book Whisperer* (2009), no longer refers to kids who are behind in reading as *struggling readers*. Instead, she calls them *developing readers*, and I like that distinction. *Struggling readers* has a negative connotation, when in truth these are readers who are behind but are still on the same trajectory as their peers. Developing readers, for whatever reason, are not reading at grade level and need some help to close the gap between where they are as readers and where they should be. They need what all readers need: continued experience reading at their instructional level.

MEETING DEVELOPING READERS WHERE THEY ARE

When children cannot read the material they are meant to learn from, something is seriously amiss. To learn, one has to participate in that learning. When the text students are given is far over their head, they can't participate. They can't read it, so they give up entirely. Not only do they miss out on what is being taught in class, but also their sense that they are stupid (which is entirely untrue) is reinforced. Worst of all, they begin to hate reading with a passion. If I were asked to do something in school every day that I couldn't do, I'd hate it too.

In order to meet the needs of these students we have to do two important things:

1. **We have to figure out where they are as readers.** We have to identify their instructional reading level and honor it. No more pretending they can read anything put before them.

2. **We have to have books at their instructional reading level available for them to read.** Doing this is not as difficult or time-consuming as it may sound, and it is a necessary step toward engaging these disenfranchised learners once and for all.

FLUENCY

Fluency (a term I use later when I discuss the running record and the five-finger rule) describes two different but related aspects of reading. One is simply the rate at which a child reads. When someone says a child is a fluent reader, they may be referring to the speed at which the child reads. More important, though, fluency generally describes how "good" readers sound. Does their voice vary as they read? Do they place emphasis in a sentence where it belongs? If children are reading in a monotone, they most likely don't understand what they are reading. If readers have to work hard to figure out each word they come upon, they lose the sense of the sentence and the reading is flat. Rasinski (2003) incorporates both of these meanings when he defines fluency as "the ability to read quickly, effortlessly, and efficiently with appropriate, meaningful expression or prosody" (p. 26). *Prosody* refers to the stress and intonation found in normal speech. I like to think of it as the music of language. When children are able to read with prosody, they understand what they are reading.

OPTIMUM READING LEVEL

There are three levels on which a child can read: independent, instructional, and frustration (see Figure 5.1):

- *Independent:* Children reading independently miss no more than two words out of a hundred (98 percent) in a passage written at their grade level.

Level	Percentage of Words Identified Correctly (Word Recognition in Context)	Outcome
Independent	98–100%	Reading at this level helps build fluency and confidence.
Instructional	90–97%	Reading at this level is where real reading gains are made.
Frustration	Below 90%	Reading at this level is fruitless and creates a dislike of reading.

Figure 5.1 Three Reading Levels

(Missing two words out of a hundred is no big deal—meaning is easily discerned. If I were to take a newspaper article and blacken out two percent of the words, you could still understand what you are reading.) These children can read a grade-level book without assistance. This is the level at which kids read for pleasure and at which, with practice, they will make gains in fluency.

- *Instructional:* The range for instructional readers varies. For most readers, missing no more than five words out of a hundred (95 percent) is optimal. They are able to read a book at this level fairly well but need help with an occasional word. (If I were to blacken out 5 percent of the words in a newspaper article, you would begin to have trouble understanding everything and would need some help.) However, readers who are more adept at constructing meaning can handle text in the 90 to 94 percent range. Children should be reading at their instructional level in class, where they can easily get the help they need identifying words they don't know. When deciding whether the 90 to 94 percent range is at a child's instructional or frustration level, it is often better to err on the side of caution and provide the student with an easier book. Listen to your students as they read. Talk to them about what they are reading. When their reading is less fluent and comprehension is dicey, an easier book is needed for gains to occur.

- *Frustration:* If children are missing more than ten words out of a hundred (90 percent), they are in too far over their heads to make any progress. The act of reading becomes too difficult to gain meaning, the task so burdensome that reading becomes work. (If I blacken out more than ten percent of the words of a newspaper article, you'd probably give up and put the paper down.) When a student decides not to read, there is no chance of moving that student forward.

QUICK AND EASY ASSESSMENTS TO IDENTIFY INSTRUCTIONAL READING LEVELS

In a perfect world, students would arrive in our classrooms accompanied by a reading inventory completed by their teacher at the end of the previous school year, and we'd know exactly where each student is as a reader. However, middle and high school teachers are responsible for numerous classes and an enormous number of students; completing a reading inventory on each student every year is impossible. We need to figure out where our students are as readers without taking up weeks of instructional time.

The Running Record

When students are reading self-selected books during daily independent reading, we can drop in on them one by one and have them privately read aloud a bit from their book. Marie Clay (1993), a renowned New Zealand educator, created the running record for situations like these—a simple chart on which we note each time the child misreads a word in a hundred-word (give or take) passage. While this doesn't tell us everything we need to know about a reader (fluency, comprehension, etc.), it does tell us whether the text fits the reader. There are numerous versions of the running record online, and quite a few sites provide in-depth directions for administering and scoring a running record.

However, I promised a quick and easy assessment, which is provided in Appendix C, Tally Sheet for Word Recognition in Context. There are a hundred squares in the chart, one for each word in a hundred-word passage. Sit down next to a child, ask her or him to read to you as you look on, and make the necessary notations. Tap your pencil against a square as a word is read correctly. When a word is misread, however, quickly put an X in that box and, if you can manage it, write down the miscue. You can also add qualitative information. For example, if a child is reading without intonation or substitutes words that are semantically correct (*house* for *home*), note these factors and take them into account when deciding what level book the child needs. Counting up the boxes that have an X in them and subtracting that number from a hundred will give you the word-recognition-in-context score. Look up that score in the reading-level chart in Figure 5.1 and identify that child's reading level. Since this isn't a full-fledged reading inventory, the level is somewhat approximate. The true test is always giving the child a book at that level and listening to them read.

The beauty of the running record is how quick and tangible it is; in six or seven minutes you have a physical record of a child's reading performance for your files. Running records can be repeated during the year as needed and the child's reading level adjusted accordingly.

The Five-Finger Rule

This assessment is even simpler, but it doesn't provide a record for your files. (Teachers who feel overwhelmed by the thought of keeping files on so many students love it!) The five-finger rule is also based on the percentages discussed above. If a child misses about five words per hundred-word passage, they are reading with 95 percent accuracy, or in the instructional range. As with a running record, the child reads aloud a hundred-word (give or take) passage as you follow along. Keeping your hands out of sight, you put a finger down each time the student misreads a word. If you have more than five fingers down when the child finishes, the book he or she is reading is probably too difficult. As always, factor in how fluent the child sounds and whether she or he can tell you a bit about what was read. However, numbers below 95 percent are a red flag.

The beauty of this method is how unobtrusive it is. Students don't see you marking a sheet of paper and therefore don't feel they are being assessed. It's not the most reliable approach, but as an on-the-fly way of getting an idea where students are as readers, it comes in very handy.

Students can apply the five-finger rule on their own when choosing a book, but it's very unreliable when they do it themselves. They catch some miscues but many more slip by because they don't realize they've read a word incorrectly. Nevertheless, knowing the five-finger rule reinforces how important it is for them to read at their instructional level.

READER PROFILE ▶ Kids Who Read Beyond Their Years

I once taught a third grader who consistently read books well beyond his life experiences. At one point he was reading *Huckleberry Finn*. He was a strong reader, to be sure, but pulling words off the page is not the same thing as understanding what we are reading.

I have two problems with kids reading a book like *Huckleberry Finn* before they're ready. First, they aren't absorbing the themes in the book: they haven't lived long enough to have had the kinds of experiences that will help them understand them. In the case of *Huckleberry Finn* they don't have the perspective to understand that the racism in the book is meant to excoriate, not sentimentalize, how African Americans were viewed at the time the book was set. (Even many high schoolers aren't ready for the book. It's much better read in college when young people know more about the world and have chalked up some life experiences.) Second, students rarely reread these books when they *are* a better fit. They say, "I already read that book and it wasn't very good." Right. But it wasn't good because they were too young to appreciate it.

So why was this third grader reading it? I talked with him about the book, sharing the above concerns, and he seemed to understand. But the following week, when I asked everyone what they were reading, this boy said, *"Moby-Dick."*

I discovered later that he wasn't picking these books, his parents were. They wanted bragging rights: "Our son's a genius." But they were pushing him in a direction he wasn't yet ready to go.

Letting the Kids In on the Secret

I am a firm believer in being honest with students. Let's face it, they know when they're not a great reader. Telling them they are makes them distrust you. Having them as an ally is far better.

At the beginning of the year I explain that in reading workshop everyone will be reading at his or her own level. Every class has a range of levels and so does this one. The secret is that by reading at their instructional level, they will steadily improve as readers and before long will be able to tackle harder books.

To introduce the concept of instructional level reading to kids, I often share this analogy. To become a great cyclist like Lance Armstrong, you start with the right equipment. You get a bike that fits you to a tee. What's most important is being able to reach the pedals. They always laugh at this, because it's so obvious. I go on to say that if you can't reach the pedals, you can't practice. If you can't practice, the likelihood of winning the Tour de France is nil. If the bike fits you, though, and you can reach the pedals, you can practice endlessly and your chances improve by about 100 percent. It's the same with reading: if you can't read the words, the book doesn't fit, and suffering through reading it isn't going to make you a better reader. But if you can read the words (like being able to reach the pedals in my analogy), you can practice and practice by reading books at that level. You will improve as a reader, guaranteed.

With the kids on board there is less likelihood that anyone will get razzed for reading an "easy" book and, frankly, some of the "easy" books are pretty terrific. It's also okay to tell them about the five-finger rule so they can use it as a tool when selecting books to read. Just remember that it's a more reliable assessment when done by an adult.

FINDING BOOKS FOR DEVELOPING READERS

The hardest part of the job—identifying instructional levels—having been accomplished, we now have to find books appropriate for the readers in our classroom. The challenge is finding books that will interest developing readers who do not look like "little kid" books. Can you imagine asking a seventh grader to walk down the halls with *Frog and Toad* tucked under her arm? That would be like wearing a sign saying *I am a giant loser*.

The good news is that over the last ten years the publishing world has adapted to the needs of the developing reader. With the increasing availability of graphic novels, novels in verse, and novels written expressly for teens who are not strong readers, the choices are far better than they once were.

Graphic Novels

Graphic novels make great easier-to-read texts. The format employs pictures as well as words to tell the story, which makes the text more accessible. Graphic novels contain all the elements of a story, presented in a visual format. For developing readers, this can be a godsend. Not every graphic novel is easy to read, however; the text in some of them can be quite daunting. They need to be evaluated carefully.

Reluctant readers are often able to finish a graphic novel in a reasonable amount of time. While this may not seem like a big deal, it is to students who have literally never finished a whole book before. Doing so gives them an extraordinary sense of accomplishment. It is this positive association with books we want for these readers.

GRAPHIC NOVELS MIDDLE SCHOOLERS CAN READ AND ENJOY

Coraline, by Neil Gaiman (2002). A wonderfully creepy tale about a little girl who goes behind the walls of her house and finds a whole other family residing there. The weird part is, they look just like her family!

The Invention of Hugo Cabret, by Brian Selznick (2007). Not exactly a graphic novel, but the story would not be complete without the pictures. The text is minimal and relatively easy to read—perfect for developing readers. It is also the basis for a fabulous feature-length film by Martin Scorsese.

Lightning Thief, by Rick Riordan (2010). The original novel is described in Chapter 1; it and some other titles in the Percy Jackson and the Olympians series are also available as graphic novels.

The Lunch Lady series, by Jarrett Krosoczka (various dates). Sadly, the stereotype of the cafeteria lady includes a hairnet and a well-placed mole. Krosoczka turns that notion upside down by making her into a superhero, with all the attendant abilities. Rather than James Bond technology, she uses repurposed kitchen gadgets (her spatula morphs into a rotor that allows her to fly up and away from trouble, for example). These books are fun as well as funny, and middle school kids love them. They are written at about a second- or third-grade level.

The Maximum Ride series, by James Patterson (various dates). Teens really love the Maximum Ride young adult novels, which prompted the publishers to reissue them as graphic novels. I recently had a student write on a survey that *Max m m R D* was his favorite book this year. (His spelling of the title made me realize again that the simpler graphic novel versions are very good things.) He said he liked it "because it's full of action." Not a bad reason for a developing middle school reader.

Rapunzel's Revenge, by Shannon Hale (2008). Takes the fairy tale of Rapunzel and amps it up with all kinds of adventure and derring-do. Rapunzel was never this wild or this funny.

Skim, by Mariko Tamaki (2008). Skim is an angsty teen who develops a crush on a female teacher at her private school. Nothing actually comes of it, but it leaves Skim questioning who she is.

Smile, by Raina Telgemeier (2010). A perfect story for middle school girls. Raina is a sixth grader who just wants to fit in. Then she trips over something and does a complete "faceplant." Her teeth take the brunt of the fall and require extensive and obvious dental work throughout the school year. How is she ever going to fit in now?

Stormbreaker (2006), *Point Blank* (2007), and *Skeleton Key* (2009), by Anthony Horowitz. A number of Horowitz's Alex Rider series have been adapted as graphic novels. Alex Rider is following in his uncle's footsteps as a spy, albeit a reluctant one. Reluctant or not, he is in the thick of it in each of these suspenseful, page-turning tales.

Yummy: The Last Days of a Southside Shorty, by G. Neri (2010). A very powerful graphic novel rendered totally in black and white. Yummy was a real kid in a gang in Chicago who, at age eleven, shoots a fourteen-year-old girl. The gang he wanted so much to belong to now sees him as a liability.

Zita the Spacegirl, by Ben Hatke (2010). When her friend accidentally gets abducted by aliens, gutsy Zita attempts to bring the friend back and finds herself a stranger on a strange planet.

Novels in Verse

The novel in free verse is another fairly quick read for developing readers. Some teachers think poetry is too challenging for developing readers, but free verse has no iambic pentameter to negotiate or rhyme schemes to pay heed to. It is sparse rather than wordy, which developing readers find more accessible. These novels generally are not lengthy and treat a wide variety of topics. Like the graphic novel, novels in verse can be finished in a relatively short time, thus giving the reader a well-deserved sense of accomplishment.

Because I Am Furniture, by Thalia Chaltas (2009). Anke lives in a house full of fear: her tyrannical father abuses her brother and sister as well as her mother. She feels worthless because her father doesn't seek her out. Playing sports and creating a life for herself outside the house empowers Anke to make a real difference in her family dynamics.

Chasing Brooklyn, by Lisa Schroeder (2010). I mentioned Schroeder's enormously popular *I Heart You, You Haunt Me* in an earlier chapter. *Chasing Brooklyn* is not a sequel, but it shares the same otherworldly quality. Brooklyn has lost her boyfriend, Lucca, and Nico has lost his brother. Both teens are being haunted, which makes them close. Is this Lucca's intention?

Chess Rumble, by G. Neri (2007). A young boy has a problem with his temper that leads him into one fight after another. He finds an outlet in a chess club that forces him to rely on his brains, not his brawn.

Far from You, by Lisa Schroeder (2009). Alice is still grieving the loss of her mother when her father remarries. When a step-sibling arrives, Alice is jealous of the baby. It takes being stranded in a snowstorm with her stepmom and stepsister for her to let go of her grief and jealousy.

Hidden, by Helen Frost (2011). Darra and Wren, teenagers at the same summer camp, eventually realize that they know one another. When she was eight, Wren was in her mother's car when it was carjacked. She escaped, but while she was hiding in the garage where the carjacker stowed the car, she came to know a little girl around her own age. That little girl was Darra.

Jinx, by Margaret Wild (2004). When one boyfriend dies, that's really hard luck. When the second one dies, there might be a question or two.

Keesha's House, by Helen Frost (2003). Keesha takes refuge in a house for teens who need a safe place. One by one, she welcomes other desperate kids who need a hand up.

Peace, Locomotion, by Jacqueline Woodson (2009). Lonnie and his sister Lili live in different foster homes. In lyrical letters to Lili, Lonnie attempts to record everything that happens as they are growing up.

Shark Girl, by Kelly Bingham (2007). Jane is a normal fifteen-year-old girl whose life changes when she is attacked by a shark. She loses most of one arm and from then on has to imagine a whole new world for herself.

Sold, by Patricia McCormick (2006). A young girl is sent from her mountain home to a big city in India to be a maid in a big house. What she doesn't know is that her stepfather has sold her into the sexual slave trade.

Who Killed Mr. Chippendale? A Mystery in Poems, by Mel Glenn (1999). Various narrators, in free verse, describe the aftermath of a high school teacher's murder.

His Name Was Raoul Wallenberg: Courage, Rescue, and Mystery During World War II, by Louise Borden (2012). The story of a famous resistance fighter from Sweden who worked in Budapest trying to save Jews from death at the hands of the Nazis—and the first nonfiction in verse I have encountered. It is nice to see such an important true story made so accessible for developing readers.

High-Interest/Low-Level Books

The best books offered for middle and high school students who are reading below grade level are three series published by Orca Books. Librarians say they are so popular it's difficult to keep them on the shelves. Best of all, these series are written at a second-, third-, or fourth-grade level. The covers look like those of any young adult novel, so no one is aware the book is "easy." The font is the same size as other middle school books as well—no giant type typical of books for younger readers.

The Orca Currents series are relatively short novels with contemporary themes that will interest readers age ten through fourteen. Topics include:

- Body image
- Mistaken identity
- A boy wanting to continue being a daredevil despite his new disability
- Activism
- Homeless teens
- Mysteries
- Humorous stories
- Popularity and revenge
- Plagiarism and music
- Gangs.

The Orca Sports series are for readers age ten and up. Sports represented include snowboarding, cheerleading, tae kwon do, mountain biking, skateboarding, spelunking, diving, hockey, football, basketball, sailing, running, horseback riding, soccer, and car racing. Sports are a huge part of our culture and are a great way to pull readers in.

Books in the Orca Soundings series are meant for ages twelve and up. The covers and topics are age appropriate. Even though they are written at lower reading levels, they are not books for elementary-age children. Topics include DNA testing, anorexia, leukemia, stalking, slam poetry, bullying, identity theft, carjacking, and steroid use.

A number of other publishers are also stepping up to the challenge of providing books for developing readers that don't talk down to them.

Saddleback Educational Publishing has a wide range of books for developing readers, including some graphic novels, at levels starting with first grade. (It is nearly impossible to write a compelling book for older children at a first-grade level, but there are times when we need one.) Topics are varied, and as reading levels increase, so does story complexity.

Lerner Books has an imprint called Darby Creek that has issued a new horror collection called Night Fall. This six-book series is set in a small New England town where things start to go a bit awry. These creepy reads, written at a fourth-grade level, are meant for students in grades 6–12.

YALSA Quick Picks for Young Adult Reluctant Readers

All middle and high school teachers should know about these lists, found on the Young Adult Library Services Association website (http://www.ala.org/yalsa/booklists/quickpicks). Going back to 1996, these lists of books are ideal for young adult reluctant readers who need to find a relevant, accessible book that is engaging right from the start. Reading levels vary, so it is best to examine the book at a bookstore or library before you purchase it. The site also features each year's top ten titles, which is most helpful when the budget is limited.

The Young Adult Library Services Association's Quick-Picks Selection Criteria

These criteria are meant as suggestions for evaluating a book on your own. Not all criteria may fit all books, but knowing what to look for is half the battle.

PHYSICAL APPEARANCE
- Cover—catchy, action-oriented, attractive, appealing, good "blurb"
- Print style—sufficiently large for enjoyable reading
- Format—appropriate and appealing balance of test and white space
- Artwork/illustrations—enticing, realistic, demonstrated diversity

STYLE
- Clear writing that easily communicates without long convoluted sentences of sophisticated vocabulary
- Acceptable literary quality and effectiveness of presentation
- Simple vocabulary but not noticeably controlled

FICTION
- High-interest "hook" in first ten pages
- Well-defined characters
- Sufficient plot to sustain interest
- Plot lines developed through dialogue and action

- Familiar themes with emotional appeal for teenagers
- Believable treatment
- Single point of view
- Touches of humor when appropriate
- Chronological order

INFORMATIONAL BOOKS
- Technical language acceptable if defined in context
- Accuracy
- Objectivity

Teaching Students to Choose Their Own Books

You won't always be looking over your students' shoulder when they choose books, so it makes good sense to help them learn to find the right book for themselves. As with anything, it takes a fair bit of support at first, but as time passes you can hand the reins over to them.

Start with the classroom library. Many teachers arrange the books by genre, by level of difficulty, or perhaps even by topic. Whatever your system, introduce and have students browse the different categories so they feel comfortable and know where to find things.

Take some books out and look at them with your students. Do they have a preference regarding number of pages? Tell them it's okay to want a short book now and then. Sometimes I look at my own bookshelf and purposefully choose a short one because that's all I have time for. But do tell them that a long book that allows them to lose themselves in the story longer is a great experience too.

Page through the book together. Is it dense with loads of text on the page and not a lot of white space? That can matter a lot to a developing reader. Be up front and say that sometimes a book like this can be off-putting. If it is, look for one that seems a bit friendlier.

What about the topic? You've nailed down the page length students are looking for and the overall accessibility of the print. Now, what would they like to read about? Do they like fantasy like Harry Potter or realistic fiction like *Diary of a Wimpy Kid*? Maybe nonfiction?

When students find a few books that interest them, show them the flap copy. Publishers use the flap copy to lure readers. It generally offers enough of a summary to let readers know what the book is about. A well-written one will pique readers' interest so they want to find out what happens. That should help students make a final choice.

You've found a book that fits the reader's preferences regarding length, print density, and topic. Now it's time for the five-finger rule. See whether the book is a good match for this student in terms of decodability. If it is, the choice is made.

After students are comfortable choosing books in the classroom library, it's time to take them to the school library and acclimate them there. After that, they'll be ready to tackle local public libraries as well.

Finally, do let students know that every now and then, despite all the care they have taken in selecting a book, they'll find it's not to their liking. When that happens (and it has to all of us), putting it back is not a bad thing. If it happens repeatedly, however, it's time to look back at how they are selecting their books because something is not right.

Getting Librarians to Stock Books for This Population

Librarians love to have books on the shelf that kids want to read. Educators all want the same thing: to help kids become lifelong readers. Librarians may not know how you feel about graphic novels or other more accessible formats and hesitate to spend their tight budget on them. Talk to your librarians and tell them what you would like to see in the library. They generally welcome suggestions, and when they see your students using the library, they'll be glad they took them!

READER PROFILE ▶ Jump-Starting Jason's Reading

Jason has been behind in reading for as long as he can remember and feels like a complete failure in school. His parents, alarmed that Jason was faltering, took him to a reading clinic where he was tutored year-round (except for holiday breaks) yet made few gains. The tutoring included repeated readings to aid his fluency, intensive word study to help build his word knowledge, and short reading selections to help him understand what he read. All these techniques are laudable, and Jason was deficient in all those areas. However, he was not given a reason to want to read. The tutoring focused on the parts of reading, but Jason was never given real books to read. The skill and drill approach did not inspire him in the slightest and infringed on his free time. He detested it.

Giving Jason real books to choose from that pique his interest, are within his reading range, and are relevant to him makes all the difference. Jason chooses a novel in verse about baseball and is thrilled when he finishes it. While he is still not caught up in reading in any big way, he now has an interest in becoming a reader. As he continues to choose books he can manage, he will find his way bit by bit. Can he still benefit from tutoring? Sure, but I doubt he needs the intensive work he had before. Keeping him reading while working on the other facets of reading in tolerable doses will brighten his future considerably.

Mallory is an easy girl to have in class. She never misbehaves or draws attention to herself. Before class she chats with her friends, bubbly and bouncy as can be. It's only when her teacher calls the class to attention that Mallory's demeanor becomes droopy and she reluctantly drags out her book. It's part of the Animal Ark series, by Ben Baglio, which is at about a fourth-grade level. She's embarrassed that she's reading such an easy book, but easy books are the only ones with which she feels comfortable. Mallory is doing the right thing for herself by reading a book at her reading level.

Still, her embarrassment is heartbreaking, and I can't resist pointing out this great series to the other students. I tell them the premise: Mandy Hope's parents operate a veterinary clinic called Animal Ark where they treat animals of all shapes and sizes. Each book features a different animal, and the author takes great pains to provide accurate information. I confide that when I was traveling in England I looked everywhere hoping to spy a hedgehog. I knew they lived under hedges and looked under any one I came across. But Ben Baglio's book *Hedgehogs in the Hall* taught me that hedgehogs are nocturnal and no matter how many hedges I peeked under during the day, I wasn't going to find one. Mallory beamed, and a few other girls went to see what other titles in the series were on the shelf.

LAST WORDS

Working with developing readers takes a little more time than working with kids who are reading at grade level. It requires finding out where the developing readers are as readers through some quick and easy assessments. Having determined their instructional reading level, it requires getting appropriate books for the classroom, the library, and the school so that developing readers can participate in what is going on in the classroom. They need the same basics of good instruction: choice in what they read, books that are relevant to their lives, and books at their reading level. If we give them books that are relevant, they will sink their teeth into reading. And they need one more thing: the sense that they can read, that they are smart, and that we expect them to flourish. After years of being the loser in class, it may take some time to convince their damaged egos that they are as competent as the next kid.

Chapter Six

Enthusiastic Middle School Readers Are Not Mythical Creatures!

hree essentials are necessary if kids are to become motivated, engaged readers primed to continue looking to books for information, vicarious experiences, entertainment, and pleasure long after they have left our classrooms. The first is a selection of books that will grab them and make them think. The second is being able to choose the books they read. The third is the availability of books at an appropriate degree of difficulty.

Choice and Relevance: Where the Rubber Meets the Road

The faculty at Warren County Middle School (WCMS) are a brave group. They wanted more for their students than their current approach was providing and decided to do something about it. But as every teacher knows, change is scary and takes time and effort. Initially I found the books for them. Once the books were in the classrooms and student interest had been aroused, the teachers began to release their control little by little and allow the kids to choose what they read. The teachers struggled, and some did better than others, but the payoff is clear. Connecting with print has become a part of the school's culture. Kids are reading more now than they ever did.

Choice is the most powerful factor in changing students' attitude toward reading. Kids engage with what they are reading if they see something of their own world in the story—if they find it relevant. Students cannot connect

The Scarlet Letter and other books typically assigned in middle school with their own world. The world of *The Scarlet Letter* is too different, too distant. There are newer books with the same theme. Middle and high school students are going to get a heck of a lot more out of *Story of a Girl*, a novel by Sara Zarr about bucking a bad reputation, than they will from *The Scarlet Letter*. What's more, because they have read and understood *Story of a Girl*, when they do read *The Scarlet Letter*, they will be more receptive to its ideas.

At WCMS, students who shied away from reading began picking up books when they were allowed to choose what they wanted to read from among books that had piqued their interest. The staff member who oversees the before-school program approached me in the hall recently and told me the new reading program is making her job easier. A fair number of students are now reading during the time before classes. Kids choosing to read in their free time is pretty exciting.

Are any of them choosing to read *The Red Badge of Courage*? No. On the other hand, most adults don't read Stephen Crane and Ernest Hemingway for pleasure. Look at people in airports—they aren't carrying books with copyrights older than they are. They are reading books by Len Deighton, Nicholas Sparks, Kathryn Stockett, and James Patterson—intriguing stories that pull them in. When is the last time you saw *A Farewell to Arms* in an airport newsstand?

ONE MORE TIME:
ONE SIZE DOES NOT FIT ALL

An equally important aspect of a strong middle school reading program is the need to honor the students' instructional reading levels. Taking the time to choose books and other reading materials that represent the wide range of readers in our classrooms is well worth the effort. If all of the reading material available in a sixth-grade classroom is written at a sixth-grade level, a fair number of the students will not be able to participate in the instruction. No teacher would knowingly put barriers in the way of students' learning. But, sadly, in a one-size-fits-all system, that's what happens. We need to provide books all our students can read.

Text Sets Honor Instructional Reading Levels

Some years back, at Thomas Harrison Middle School, in Harrisonburg, Virginia, two extraordinary teachers put their heads together and came up with a way to make it clear to the faculty and administration that there were students who could not read the texts being issued to them each year. Loretta Stewart, an outstanding reading specialist, and Peggy McIntyre, a remarkable librarian, first examined students' end-of-year reading scores. Then they looked at the reading levels at which the texts in their building were written. They found a startling mismatch between what the kids could read and what they were given to read. They presented their findings to the language arts supervisor, Linda Bland, who funded Loretta and Peggy's project to create text sets for every discipline taught in the school.

Peggy and Loretta found books on every topic in their middle school curriculum, made sure a range of reading levels were represented (beginning, grades K–1; transitional, grades 2–3, and competent through proficient, grades 4–8), and put each text set in its own labeled, bar-coded tub. Teachers could check out these tubs (which were stored in an anteroom) from the library. With one of these tubs in the classroom, every child could be reading material at his or her instructional reading level. No one would become frustrated and turned off. All students became better readers by practicing reading at their instruction level.

AN EXAMPLE TEXT SET ON ABRAHAM LINCOLN

Beginning Readers (Grades K–1)
Abe Lincoln's Hat, by Martha Brenner, illustrated by Donald Cook (1994)

Billy and the Rebel, by Deborah Hopkinson, illustrated by Brian Floca (2005)

Abe Lincoln and the Muddy Pig, by Stephen Krensky (2002)

Abe Lincoln Remembers, by Ann Turner, illustrated by Wendell Minor (2003)

Transitional Readers (Grades 2–3)
Lincoln and Douglass: An American Friendship, by Nikki Giovanni, illustrated by Bryan Collier (2008)

Abe Lincoln Crosses a Creek: A Tall, Thin Tale (Introducing His Forgotten Frontier Friend), by Deborah Hopkinson, illustrated by John Hendrix (2008)

Who Was Abraham Lincoln?, by Janet Pascal, illustrated by John O'Brien (2008)

Abe's Honest Words, by Doreen Rappaport, illustrated by Kadir Nelson (2008)

Lincoln and His Boys, by Rosemary Wells, illustrated by P. J. Lynch (2009)

Abe Lincoln: The Boy Who Loved Books, by Kay Winters, illustrated by Nancy Carpenter (2002)

Competent Through Proficient Readers (Grades 4–8)
Lincoln: A Photobiography, by Russell Freedman (1987)

Lincoln Through the Lens: How Photography Revealed and Shaped an Extraordinary Life, by Martin W. Sandler (2008)

Chasing Lincoln's Killer: The Search for John Wilkes Booth, by James Swanson (2009)

The Gettysburg Address, by Abraham Lincoln, illustrated by Michael McCurdy (1998)

Acquiring and Identifying Books

Stocking the bookshelves in our classrooms randomly is not the way to go. We have to choose wisely so that students aren't overwhelmed with endless choices and end up choosing badly. We need to choose what we think they will like and what we think is worthwhile. Choice within parameters is a good thing. We can't do this all on our own; we didn't take a book selection course in college. But we do have people around us who can help.

Librarians. As a first step consult your school librarian. If she is familiar with books for middle schoolers, pick her brain for some great titles. If she can't help, your classroom library may end up being better stocked with teen reads than the school library; in that case you can diplomatically let her know what your students are reading. The local public librarian is also a resource. A good public library system has a teen specialist, and that person will be able to make suggestions based on circulation numbers. You can't get more reliable information than that.

Bookstores. Browsing the local bookstore(s) is free. Ask the clerks what books for teens are selling. Employees in the big chains probably won't know, but local independent booksellers will.

The Internet. Websites specializing in teen books or graphic novels list lots of titles. Look up likely titles on barnesandnoble.com or amazon.com and check the suggested age range. The reading level may not be the same but age appropriateness is important. A book that is age appropriate for your grade level is less likely to be the target of a censorship challenge. Read a bit about the book online so you have a sense of whether a particular book will fit into your classroom.

BOOKLISTS ON THE INTERNET

Capitol Choices (www.capitolchoices.org/welcome). Capitol Choices is an online discussion group that you can participate in or simply shadow. Newly published books are nominated by group members and discussed at a monthly meeting, the transcript of which is available online. There are also yearly lists of noteworthy books from 1996 to the present. Titles for reluctant readers (things like *Captain Underpants*) aren't on the lists, but many outstanding titles are.

ALA's Teens' Top Ten (www.ala.org/yalsa/teenstopten). YALSA, the teen arm of the American Library Association, distributes great information. The Teens' Top Ten list identifies the most popular books teens are reading each year.

Best Fiction for Young Adults (www.ala.org/yalsa/bfya/2012). Another reliable YALSA list of what teens are really reading.

Amazon.com has a link to the New York Times Bestseller List for Teens.

Good Reads (www.goodreads.com). You have to join this site (doing so is free), but once you are a member, you have access to all kinds of lists—Rockin' Books Read as a Child, Best Epic Fantasy, Best Young Adult Books, Books That Should Be Made into Movies, and What to Read Next, to name a few. You'll get some great ideas not only for your classroom but also for your own reading.

As you consult librarians, check out websites, and browse bookstores, you'll encounter some of the same titles and authors again and again. That's a sign kids are reading those books. Also check out other books by popular authors. If your students like the novel *No More Dead Dogs*, by Gordon Korman, for example, look for other Korman titles to add to your library.

Obtaining Books

In cash-strapped school districts it's hard to find the money to purchase trade books. Here are a few tricks that can help:

- Ask your principal for support. Yes, budgets are tight, but districts always seem to come up with money when necessary. It's worth explaining your plans and seeing whether the principal can find some funds.

- Apply for grants offered by your school district, local government departments, or professional organizations. You can often find sources of funding through an Internet search.

- Use book fairs. Each school uses book fair money in different ways. Put in a request that the sixth grade gets it this year, seventh grade next year, and so on.

- Book fairs often feature teacher "wish lists." Parents can purchase these books for your classroom as a nod to your good work in the classroom.

- Use book clubs in your classroom. These clubs get books into the hands of your kids at discounted prices and earn you much-needed bonus points for even more books.

- Haunt used bookstores and stores that sell remaindered books.

- Ask the parent-teacher organization to sponsor a bake sale, pizza night, silent auction, or anything else you can think of to raise funds for books.

- If a parent offers monetary help, ask for a gift certificate to a bookstore and use it to buy more books for your classroom.

A Picture Is Worth a Thousand Words

The biggest change at WCMS has been in teachers' and students' attitudes toward reading. The teachers are thrilled by how much more their students are reading. Rebecca Webster, who started the ball rolling toward change, sent me an amazing photo: it shows her students standing in front of the school, each proudly holding a piece of paper on which is written the number of books he or she read so far this year. The lowest number I can spot is 10, and I'm sure that's a big increase for that student. More evident, though, are numbers like 55, 32, 40, 28, and 71. That range is typical when kids are reading relevant books of their own choosing. How can we be disappointed in our approach when we get results like these?

It's great to watch the enthusiasm of the WCMS teachers for what they are reading spill over to their students. In a class, one day I spied two boys reading Markus Zusak's *The Book Thief*, an extraordinary (and lengthy) book about a young girl during the Nazi reign in Germany and how she interprets what is going on around her. It's a somewhat depressing topic and a daunting read, so I was surprised to see it on the boys' desks. I stopped and chatted with them about the book. They mentioned a great many details and said how much they were enjoying it. Clearly, they were engaged. I then asked what had prompted them to read it. They told me their teacher, Mrs. Dusing, always reads when they do and tells them about what she is reading. Her description of *The Book Thief* made them decide they had to read it themselves.

I love that Jamie Dusing reads while her students do. That kind of modeling is vital and makes a big impact. I love that she tells the class about the books she reads. She is helping turn her classroom into a literate community by making talk about books commonplace. I also love that she explores the same topic her kids are reading about. She knows it's the best way to motivate them. These students have a teacher who loves to read, is reading books on the same topics they're reading about, and tells them when she's found a good one.

When I talk with a group of teachers, I often start by asking what children's or young adult book they've read recently that they really enjoyed. In most cases, there are a few uncomfortable moments before only two or three hands go up. How can we motivate kids to read when we don't read ourselves and know very little about books geared to their abilities and interests? It starts with us.

Years ago I received a compliment I still treasure. A student said, "Mrs. Kindig, you make every book sound good!" What Jacob didn't know is that I choose the books I give book talks on carefully. I never try to sell students something I don't like myself. I read quite a bit and when I find something I think my students will like, I tell them about it. It's easy to make books sound good when I love them too. Reading children's books is a pleasure, and sharing the books with them is as rewarding as it gets.

THE ENVELOPE, PLEASE

At the end of the final year of my consultancy I gave the WCMS teachers a chance to describe what they thought about this new approach in an end-of-the-year questionnaire. Eighty-five percent said they now fully implement the reading workshop approach—that is, they have moved away from reading archaic books toward reading current young adult literature.

Positives

The teachers I surveyed were thrilled to report that their kids were reading more, were reading widely, and were feeling empowered as readers. The teachers felt that their work in finding books that the students could read and that the students were interested in reading had paid off: they noted dramatic improvements in stamina, fluency, and willingness to read and participate in class. *Their students had become passionate readers. They were choosing to read, and they were drawing meaning from what they were reading. Reading had become part of their lives.* Isn't that every language arts teacher's goal?

Concerns

Naturally, I also asked about the teachers' concerns about this new approach. While the issues that they identified are understandable, they're not insurmountable. The first concern was grading: it can be scary to let go of quizzes if they're a tool you've used for years. We know that the old ten-question quizzes are an unreliable measure of comprehension, but they can seem like a useful tool when a teacher is faced with assessing comprehension while kids are reading a wide variety of books. There are other avenues to explore, though. Consider having kids blog about their book or create and share a PowerPoint presentation about it with their class; this will tell us in an instant whether they "get" the book or not.

Other issues that the teachers identified involved the nuts and bolts of running a reading workshop: keeping track of what kids are reading, monitoring whether the kids understand what they are reading, and managing time. Resources like Nancie Atwell's *In the Middle* (1987) and Laura Robb's *Teaching Reading in Middle School* (2000) are packed with management tools and forms for doing this. We don't have to create everything ourselves: there's no need to reinvent the wheel.

Finally, the teachers admitted that while they had seen wonderful gains in their classes, not every student had fallen in love with reading. Reluctant readers are a challenge—and they will be in any reading approach. But there is a far better chance of engaging these kids in real books than in textbooks they can't even read. By middle school, these readers have sharpened their coping and avoidance skills. They see themselves as nonreaders and don't trust they will ever be readers. We need to not only find the right books for them but also make them feel they can be successful.

HOW THE KIDS SEE IT

Students had a lot to say about how reading has changed in their school. Predictably there were some gripers. A few said they were bored (what kid doesn't say this at one time or another?), some complained that too much time was spent reading, and one lamented that reading was required even when he didn't love the book he had chosen (oh, the horror!). These reluctant readers were certainly heard. Overall, though, they were in a small minority. For example, when I asked the students if their time spent reading had increased, out of eighty-eight responses only ten said no.

The majority of the students responded with incredible enthusiasm, many of them requesting more reading time in class. These kids, typical middle schoolers who are struggling with their own identities and initial attempts at independence, were energized by the trust their teachers had placed in them: their teachers had not only let them choose their own reading materials, they'd allowed them to read stretched out on the rug and given them an environment in which they could share their thoughts. The students had also begun to feel a sense of agency in their reading, and they reported reading more than they had before. The positive changes were remarkable. Here are some of the comments the students made when I asked what they liked about reading that year:

- "The selection of books."
- "When Jamie tells Landon she has leukemia." (Sharing a particular aspect of a book is powerful signal of engagement!)

- "We got to pick what we wanted to read."
- "Chillin.'" (What a great vibe: in the zone, reading stretched out on a rug—most assuredly chillin'!)
- "I found my favorite author."
- "I could express my opinions about reading."
- "We could read on the rug and there were lots of books."
- "It gives you time to actually read your book."
- "I read now a lot more than I used to."
- "How I got help finding my books."
- "I think we should just do book talks and no projects, but other than that, I like it."
- "We should share about books more."
- "Have two days of just reading in class."
- "Read to the class a little more."
- "More projects based on books."
- "The whole class sharing books, more reading time."

I love these comments. Kids are finding authors they like, they love being able to choose what they read, they are talking about books, and they like sharing what they learn from books.

What Would Make Reading Class Better?

I asked the kids what we could do differently when teaching reading and was stunned by what some of them suggested: they wanted more time to read, more projects (rather than quizzes and tests), and an even larger selection of books. Once they'd had a taste of self-direction and open-ended responses, they wanted more! Imagine what an advantage these kids will have in the world once they're out of school: they'll have experience in taking on complex tasks that require serious thought, not just filling in the right answer on a quiz.

- "Give more projects and share books more. Other than that, I really loved class this year. ☺"
- "Less practice on reading-strategy tests. The Standards of Learning tests are hard enough. And practicing with those stories just is too much. Thanks. ☺"
- "More time, more books, more group activities, more projects, more group projects."

- "Have a larger selection of books."
- "We should share about books more."
- "Have more reading time."
- "Read to the class a little more."
- "More projects based on books."
- "Share books with the whole class, more reading time."

Genre Preferences

At my request, students listed their favorite genres—important information. They like realistic fiction best. This isn't surprising; they love books that are relevant to them. Close behind are fantasy and graphic novels. (They don't see themselves in historical fiction novels, so they read that genre the least.)

They put science fiction way down on their list as well, yet eat up dystopian fantasies about what happens when societies strive to create utopias and fail. They see these books as fantasy rather than science fiction, and in truth they straddle both genres.

SOME GOOD STORIES ABOUT DYSTOPIAS

The Hunger Games trilogy, by Suzanne Collins (various dates)
Divergent, by Veronica Roth (2011)
The City of Ember series, by Jeanne DuPrau (various dates)
The Chaos Walking series, by Patrick Ness (various dates)
Life As We Knew It, by Susan Beth Pfeffer (2006)
How I Live Now, by Meg Rosoff (2004)
The Forest of Hands and Teeth, by Carrie Ryan (2010)
Incarceron, by Catherine Fisher (2010)
The House of the Scorpion, by Nancy Farmer (2002)
Unwind, by Neal Shusterman (2007)
Rash, by Pete Hautman (2006)
Feed, by M. T. Anderson (2002)
The Uglies series, by Scott Westerfeld (various dates)
The Giver, by Lois Lowry (1993)

Graphic novels are not a genre but rather a format. I am not at all surprised to see them up at the top of the preference list. Graphic novels cover all genres and they are ideal for this generation that has grown up with visuals.

Mysteries and nonfiction fall in the middle of the list. Mysteries are great for unengaged readers because the genre is geared to keep the reader turning the pages. I would have liked nonfiction to be higher on the list, but we spend more time on fiction, so we shouldn't be surprised. I think that making nonfiction more available to students will change their feelings about it.

LAST WORDS

My survey was not empirical. I was simply documenting as best I could the changes that took place at WCMS. My work there began in spring, 2010, when I introduced the concept of reading workshop and provided books for students to read, and several teachers began implementing the reading program. The major push, with most teachers on board, took place during the 2010–11 school year. In spring, 2011, students' scores on the Standards of Learning tests didn't significantly improve or weaken. Since the teachers were still learning to balance the reading and direct instruction (something they continue to work on), that seemed logical. Now most of the kids are reading like crazy, but some reluctant readers are still digging in their heels. We have made a lot of headway and continue to try to reach the students who did not jump onboard immediately.

We do know that choice, relevance, and honoring instructional levels have changed the WCMS students' attitudes about reading and how much they read. The SOL tests—or any standardized test—don't address this issue. By turning so many kids on to reading, we have succeeded in our goal to help them become lifelong learners. If they continue reading at this pace and with this enthusiasm, their futures look bright.

Appendix A

Initial Warren County Middle School Survey

When I started visiting Warren County Middle School, I knew I couldn't possibly buy books for their readers workshop without knowing a lot more about the kids they served. This survey helped me get a handle on where the kids were as readers, what their attitudes about reading were, and what their likes and dislikes were.

Reading Survey: Grades 6–8

Introduction: Do you like to talk with your friends and find out what is going on with them? Hear what they did over the weekend—that sort of thing? *It's kind of like hearing and telling stories, isn't it?*

1. What about stories in books? Do you like hearing books read aloud to you?

2. Can you tell me one that you really loved when it was read aloud to you?

   Who read it to you?

3. What do you think of when you see or hear the word *reading*?

4. Not all books are fiction or stories, are they? Do you like to hear or read nonfiction? You know, books about real things? Can you tell me a nonfiction book you really liked?

5. Do you have time to read in school? What kinds of things do you like to read about (i.e., sports, pets, adventures, relationships, mysteries, etc.)?

6. Do you have free choice in what you read at school, or is all reading assigned? If it's assigned, what was the last book that was assigned to you? Did you like it?

7. When a teacher says you're going to be starting a new book, what words would you use to describe how you usually feel?
   Explain why.

   (Examples of words: *curious, excited, anxious, uncertain, irritated, angry*)

8. Do you read at home? What kinds of books?

9. What's the last book you read that you liked?

10. Do you like reading? If you don't like reading, what would it take for you to like it?

11. How much time do you spend on the Internet each day? What kinds of things do you read on the Internet?

12. What are some of the things that you do in your free time?

100 Picture Books for Older Readers

Because I use picture books with older students all the time, I am often asked for a list of good books for that purpose. I finally sat down and put this list together.

Alexander, Elizabeth, Marilyn Nelson, and Floyd Cooper. *Miss Crandall's School for Young Ladies and Little Misses of Color: Poems.* Honesdale, PA: Wordsong, 2007.

Angelou, Maya, Edwin Graves Wilson, and Jerome Lagarrigue. *Poetry for Young People.* New York: Sterling, 2007.

Asch, Frank, and Devin Asch. *Mr. Maxwell's Mouse.* Toronto: Kids Can Press, 2004.

Bedard, Michael, Barbara Cooney, and Lynn Braswell. *Emily.* New York: Delacorte Press, 1992.

Brown, Don. *America Is Under Attack: September 11, 2001: The Day the Towers Fell.* New York: Roaring Brook Press, 2011.

Bryant, Jennifer, and Melissa Sweet. *A River of Words: The Story of William Carlos Williams.* Grand Rapids, MI: Eerdmans Books for Young Readers, 2008.

Buehner, Caralyn, and Mark Buehner. *Fanny's Dream.* New York: Dial Books for Young Readers, 1996.

Bunting, Eve, and Chris K. Soentpiet. *So Far from the Sea.* New York: Clarion Books, 1998.

Bunting, Eve, and David Diaz. *Smoky Night.* San Diego: Harcourt Brace, 1994.

Bunting, Eve, and James Ransome. *Your Move.* San Diego: Harcourt Brace, 1998.

Bunting, Eve, and Stephen Gammell. *Terrible Things: An Allegory of the Holocaust.* Philadelphia: Jewish Publication Society, 1989.

Coerr, Eleanor, Ed Young, and Eleanor Coerr. *Sadako.* New York: Putnam, 1993.

Coleman, Evelyn, and Tyrone Geter. *White Socks Only.* Morton Grove, IL: Whitman, 1996.

Coles, Robert, and George Ford. *The Story of Ruby Bridges.* New York: Scholastic, 1995.

Cooney, Barbara. *Eleanor.* New York: Viking, 1996.

Crew, Gary, and Steven Woolman. *The Watertower.* Brooklyn, NY: Crocodile Books, 1998.

Deedy, Carmen Agra, and Henri Sørensen. *The Yellow Star: The Legend of King Christian X of Denmark.* Atlanta: Peachtree, 2000.

Ehrlich, Amy, and Wendell Minor. *Rachel: The Story of Rachel Carson.* San Diego: Harcourt, 2003.

Fleischman, Paul, and Kevin Hawkes. *Weslandia.* Cambridge, MA: Candlewick Press, 1999.

Gaiman, Neil, and Dave McKean. *The Day I Swapped My Dad for Two Goldfish.* New York: HarperCollins Children's Books, 2004.

Gaiman, Neil, and Dave McKean. *The Wolves in the Walls.* New York: Harper-Collins, 2003.

Garland, Sherry, and Tatsuro Kiuchi. *The Lotus Seed.* San Diego: Harcourt Brace Jovanovich, 1993.

Gerstein, Mordicai. *The Man Who Walked Between the Towers.* Brookfield, CT: Roaring Brook Press, 2003.

Golenbock, Peter, and Paul Bacon. *Teammates.* San Diego: Harcourt Brace Jovanovich, 1990.

Gravett, Emily. *Wolves.* New York: Simon & Schuster Books for Young Readers, 2006.

Greenberg, Jan, Sandra Jordan, and Brian Floca. *Ballet for Martha: Making Appalachian Spring.* New York: RB/Flash Point, 2010.

Heide, Florence Parry, Judith Heide Gilliland, and Ted Lewin. *Sami and the Time of the Troubles.* New York: Clarion Books, 1992.

Hopkinson, Deborah, and James Ransome. *Sky Boys: How They Built the Empire State Building.* New York: Atheneum Books for Young Readers, 2006.

Howitt, Mary Botham, and Tony DiTerlizzi. *The Spider and the Fly.* New York: Simon & Schuster Books for Young Readers, 2002.

Hughes, Langston. *Poetry for Young People.* New York: Sterling Publishing, 2006.

Hunter, Sara Hoagland, and Julia Miner. *The Unbreakable Code.* Flagstaff, AZ: Northland, 1996.

Innocenti, Roberto. *Rose Blanche.* Mankato, MN: Creative Education, 1985.

Johnson, D. B. *Henry Hikes to Fitchburg.* Boston: Houghton Mifflin, 2000.

Kerley, Barbara, and Brian Selznick. *Walt Whitman: Words for America.* New York: Scholastic Press, 2004.

Kodama, Tatsuharu, and Noriyuki Ando. *Shin's Tricycle*. New York: Walker, 1995.

Krull, Kathleen, and Yuyi Morales. *Harvesting Hope: The Story of Cesar Chavez*. San Diego: Harcourt, 2003.

Lawrence, Jacob. *Harriet and the Promised Land*. New York: Simon & Schuster Books for Young Readers, 1993.

Levine, Ellen, and Kadir Nelson. *Henry's Freedom Box*. New York: Scholastic Press, 2007.

Lincoln, Abraham, and Michael McCurdy. *The Gettysburg Address*. Boston: Houghton Mifflin, 1995.

Littlesugar, Amy, and Floyd Cooper. *Freedom School, Yes!* New York: Philomel Books, 2001.

Lowry, Lois, and Bagram Ibatoulline. *Crow Call*. New York: Scholastic Press, 2009.

Lyon, George Ella, and Peter Catalanotto. *Cecil's Story*. New York: Orchard Books, 1991.

Martin, Jacqueline Briggs, and Mary Azarian. *Snowflake Bentley*. Boston: Houghton Mifflin, 1998.

Martin, Rafe, and David Shannon. *The Rough-Face Girl*. New York: G. P. Putnam's Sons, 1992.

McCully, Emily Arnold. *The Ballot Box Battle*. New York: Knopf, 1996.

McCully, Emily Arnold. *The Bobbin Girl*. New York: Dial Books for Young Readers, 1996.

McDonough, Yona Zeldis, and Bethanne Andersen. *Louisa: The Life of Louisa May Alcott*. New York: Henry Holt, 2009.

McGill, Alice, and Chris K. Soentpiet. *Molly Bannaky*. Boston, MA: Houghton Mifflin, 1999.

Miller, William, and R. Gregory Christie. *Richard Wright and the Library Card*. New York: Lee & Low, 1997.

Mitchell, Margaree King, and James Ransome. *Uncle Jed's Barbershop*. New York: Simon & Schuster Books for Young Readers, 1993.

Mochizuki, Ken, and Dom Lee. *Baseball Saved Us*. New York: Lee & Low, 1993.

Mochizuki, Ken, and Dom Lee. *Passage to Freedom: The Sugihara Story*. New York: Lee & Low, 1997.

Morrison, Toni. *Remember: The Journey to School Integration*. Boston: Houghton Mifflin, 2004.

Moser, Barry. *Tucker Pfeffercorn: An Old Story Retold*. Boston: Little, Brown, 1994.

Myers, Walter Dean, and Ann Grifalconi. *Patrol*. New York: HarperCollins, 2002.

Nelson, Kadir. *We Are the Ship: The Story of Negro League Baseball*. New York: Jump at the Sun/Hyperion Books for Children, 2008.

Nelson, Marilyn, and Philippe Lardy. *A Wreath for Emmett Till*. Boston: Houghton Mifflin, 2005.

Nelson, Vaunda Micheaux, and R. Gregory Christie. *Bad News for Outlaws: The Remarkable Life of Bass Reeves, Deputy U.S. Marshal*. Minneapolis: Carolrhoda Books, 2009.

Novesky, Amy, and David Diaz. *Me, Frida*. New York: Abrams Books for Young Readers, 2010.

Oppenheim, Shulamith Levey, and Ronald Himler. *The Lily Cupboard*. New York: HarperCollins, 1992.

Polacco, Patricia. *Pink and Say*. New York: Philomel Books, 1994.

Prelutsky, Jack, and Carin Berger. *Behold the Bold Umbrellaphant: And Other Poems*. New York: Greenwillow Books, 2006.

Prelutsky, Jack, and Peter Sís. *Scranimals*. New York: Greenwillow Books, 2002.

Ryan, Pam Muñoz, and Brian Selznick. *Amelia and Eleanor Go for a Ride: Based on a True Story*. New York: Scholastic Press, 1999.

Ryan, Pam Muñoz, and Brian Selznick. *When Marian Sang: The True Recital of Marian Anderson*. New York: Scholastic Press, 2002.

Scieszka, Jon, and Lane Smith. *Math Curse*. New York: Viking, 1995.

Scieszka, Jon, and Lane Smith. *Science Verse*. New York: Viking, 2004.

Scieszka, Jon, and Lane Smith. *Seen Art?* New York: Viking, 2005.

Scieszka, Jon, and Lane Smith. *Squids Will Be Squids: Fresh Morals, Beastly Fables*. New York: Viking, 1998.

Scieszka, Jon, and Lane Smith. *The Stinky Cheese Man*. New York: Penguin Books, 1992.

Scieszka, Jon, and Lane Smith. *The True Story of the 3 Little Pigs!* New York: Viking Kestrel, 1989.

Scieszka, Jon, and Steve Johnson. *The Frog Prince, Continued*. New York: Viking, 1991.

Selznick, Brian. *The Invention of Hugo Cabret: A Novel in Words and Pictures*. New York: Scholastic Press, 2007.

Seuss, Dr. *The Lorax*. New York: Random House, 1971.

Shetterly, Robert. *Americans Who Tell the Truth*. New York: Dutton Children's Books, 2005.

Sisulu, Elinor, and Sharon Wilson. *The Day Gogo Went to Vote: South Africa, April 1994*. Boston: Little, Brown, 1996.

Smith, Lane. *It's a Book*. New York: Roaring Brook Press, 2010.

Smith, Lane. *John, Paul, George & Ben*. New York: Hyperion Books for Children, 2006.

Sís, Peter. *The Wall: Growing Up Behind the Iron Curtain*. New York: Farrar, Straus & Giroux, 2007.

Sís, Peter, and Lilian Rosenstreich. *Starry Messenger: A Book Depicting the Life of a Famous Scientist, Mathematician, Astronomer, Philosopher, Physicist, Galileo Galilei*. New York: Farrar, Straus & Giroux, 1996.

Stanley, Diane, and Peter Vennema. *Bard of Avon: The Story of William Shakespeare*. New York: Morrow Junior Books, 1992.

Swope, Sam, and Barry Root. *The Araboolies of Liberty Street*. New York: Potter, 1989.

Tan, Shaun. *The Arrival*. New York: Arthur A. Levine Books, 2007.

Tan, Shaun. *Tales from Outer Suburbia*. New York: Arthur A. Levine Books, 2009.

Teague, Mark. *Dear Mrs. LaRue: Letters from Obedience School*. New York: Scholastic Press, 2002.

Tsuchiya, Yukio, and Ted Lewin. *Faithful Elephants: A True Story of Animals, People, and War*. Boston: Houghton Mifflin, 1988.

Tunnell, Michael O., and Ted Rand. *Mailing May*. New York: Greenwillow Books, 1997.

Turner, Ann Warren, and Ronald Himler. *Nettie's Trip South*. New York: Macmillan, 1987.

Van, Allsburg Chris. *The Mysteries of Harris Burdick*. Boston: Houghton Mifflin, 1984.

Van, Allsburg Chris. *The Stranger*. Boston: Houghton Mifflin, 1986.

Van, Allsburg Chris. *The Sweetest Fig*. Boston: Houghton Mifflin, 1993.

Van, Allsburg Chris. *The Widow's Broom*. Boston: Houghton Mifflin, 1992.

Weatherford, Carole Boston. *Birmingham, 1963*. Honesdale, PA: Wordsong, 2007.

Weatherford, Carole Boston, and Jerome Lagarrigue. *Freedom on the Menu: The Greensboro Sit-ins*. New York: Dial Books for Young Readers, 2005.

Wild, Margaret, and Anne Spudvilas. *Woolvs in the Sitee*. Victoria, Australia: Viking, 2006.

Wiles, Deborah, and Jerome Lagarrigue. *Freedom Summer*. New York: Atheneum Books for Young Readers, 2001.

Winter, Jonah, and François Roca. *Muhammad Ali: Champion of the World*. New York: Schwartz & Wade Books, 2007.

Wisniewski, David, and Lee Salsbery. *Golem*. New York: Clarion Books, 1996.

Yin, and Chris K. Soentpiet. *Coolies*. New York: Philomel Books, 2001.

Yolen, Jane, and David Shannon. *Encounter*. San Diego: Harcourt Brace Jovanovich, 1992.

$\mathcal{A}$ppendix C

Tally Sheet for Word Recognition in Context

A quick and easy way to see how well a student is decoding text is to do a running record. Marie Clay came up with the idea and numerous people have put their spin on it. I made it very simple with this straightforward chart that you can use to record errors in a 100-word passage. See Chapter 5 for a full explanation.

How to Become a Children's Literature Expert in Fifteen Easy Steps

1. Read! Read! Read!

2. One of the most reliable sources for recommendations is your librarian. Introduce yourself to the local librarian and befriend your school librarian. Ask them to recommend some children's books that would be of interest to the children that you teach.

3. Find out what the children themselves are reading. *Harry Potter and the Sorcerer's Stone* didn't become a bestseller because teachers recommended it. Kids discovered it, fell in love with it, and told their friends about it.

4. Visit bookstores and browse the children's department. Ask a knowledgeable bookseller for some books that they feel you shouldn't miss (this is more productive in an independent bookstore). Remember, it's not always the ones being displayed up front.

5. Talk to your librarian and ask him or her to booktalk five or six books once a month at a faculty meeting. In a few short booktalks, your librarian can identify a great poetry book, a great nonfiction book, a great chapter book, a great transitional chapter book, a great beginning reader, and a great picture book. You will find that it will pique faculty interest in books and it will send a strong message that the faculty cares enough about literacy to encourage such sharing in faculty meetings. Not to mention that it will likely be the highlight of the faculty meeting!

6. Notice where the "Best of" lists in journals are published and when. For instance, *School Library Journal* has a best of the year list in their December issue. *The Reading Teacher* features their "Children's Choices" list in October. *The Bulletin of the Center for Children's Books* showcases their Bulletin Blue Ribbons list in the January issue. Your librarian should be able to let you know when each of these appears and, perhaps, would be willing to Xerox one and put it in your box.

7. Subscribe to *Book Links*, a journal for educators and anyone else interested in good children's books. It offers great ideas on books and the use of them in the classroom. Their website is listed on page 115.

8. Use the Internet and begin to look at different sites for book recommendations. Some suggestions are Capitol Choices, American Library Association, State Award sites, the International Reading Association, and Guys Read. URLs are listed on page 115.

9. Seek out your state reading association's list. Plan on using it in your class-room and, if possible, schoolwide. These lists are generally put together to turn children on to books they might have otherwise missed. The selections tend to be ones that children enjoy and might motivate them to read more and more. You will get lots of great ideas from those lists. The Virginia Young Readers list can be found at the Virginia State Reading Association's website listed on page 115. A website that contains links to all of the state awards can be found at Cynthia Leitich-Smith's website (see page 115).

10. Ask your librarian to create a book cart of children's books that he or she thinks would be worthwhile summer reading for your faculty. An honor system checkout is all that is needed, and you have some great books to read at the pool all summer. The added benefit is that the school already owns these books, so you can recommend them to children knowing that they will be readily available to them.

11. Take advantage of the book clubs and book fairs from Scholastic and local national and independent booksellers. The book clubs are a great source for inexpensive books for your classroom. Check with your librarian for the strong titles and stock up.

12. Go to regional, state, and national conferences where authors are featured. Bring your signed books back to share with the children and tell them what you learned about the author. This brings the authors alive to them and makes them want to read that author's work.

13. Check out the American Library Association's website (see page 115), which has complete lists of Newbery, Caldecott, Coretta Scott King, and Printz awards, among others. Do keep in mind, however, that some of the Newbery titles can be a bit dated. Remember, in 1952 *Secret of the Andes* by Ann Nolan Clark won the Newbery. While certainly a strong book, the book we all remember from that year is the Honor book: *Charlotte's Web* by E. B. White.

14. Start a children's book discussion group in your school for faculty or parents. Reading a book a month as a faculty is a wonderful way to commit yourself to reading. The discussion that follows will help you to decide whether this book is one that you would want to use with your students. Further, it sharpens your discussion skills as well as book selection skills. Parents are often eager to be part of their child's schooling, and reading good books together is a positive way to make the home-school connection.

15. Linda Sue Park, author of the 2002 Newbery Award winner, *A Single Shard*, said in her Newbery acceptance speech that her father regularly took her and her siblings to the library when she was a child. A Korean

immigrant and unable to speak English very well, he made it his business to find out what American children were reading so that his children might have the same advantages. Years later, she asked him where he had gotten his ideas and he showed her an accordion file of book lists he had clipped from newspapers or found in libraries so that he had ideas at the ready. In the days of the Internet, lists such as these are at your fingertips. In the Parks' case, those lists helped form a Newbery Award winner. What can it do for your children?

Recommended Websites

American Library Association: www.ala.org

Book Links: www.ala.org/booklinks

Capitol Choices: www.capitolchoices.org

Children's Literature Web Guide: www.acs.ucalgary.ca/~dkbrown/index.html

Guys Read: www.guysread.com

International Reading Association: www.reading.org

Cynthia Leitich-Smith (State awards information):
www.cynthialeitichsmith.com.

Virginia Readers' Choice: http://www.vsra.org/VRCindex.html

Recommended Blogs

The following are some blogs that I read regularly that talk about both children's and adolescent literature. Blogs can be a fun way to hear about new books. Each blog has its own personality and features somewhat different books. Take a peek and see what you think.

Blue Rose Girls: http://bluerosegirls.blogspot.com/

A Chair, a Fireplace, and a Tea Cozy:
http://blog.schoollibraryjournal.com/teacozy

Educating Alice: http://medinger.wordpress.com/

A Fuse #8 Production: http://blog.schoollibraryjournal.com/afuse8production/

Jacket Knack: http://jacketknack.blogspot.com/

Reading Rants!: www.readingrants.org/

Seven Impossible Things Before Breakfast: www.blaine.org/sevenimpossible
things/

Waking Brain Cells: http://wakingbraincells.com/

Appendix E

Bibliographies of Works by Featured Authors

Susan Campbell Bartoletti

Bartoletti, Susan Campbell. *Black Potatoes: The Story of the Great Irish Famine, 1845-1850*. Boston: Houghton Mifflin, 2001.

Bartoletti, Susan Campbell. *The Boy Who Dared*. New York: Scholastic, 2008.

Bartoletti, Susan Campbell. *A Coal Miner's Bride: The Diary of Anetka Kaminska*. New York: Scholastic, 2000.

Bartoletti, Susan Campbell. *Growing Up in Coal Country*. Boston: Houghton Mifflin, 1996.

Bartoletti, Susan Campbell. *Hitler Youth: Growing Up in Hitler's Shadow*. New York: Scholastic Nonfiction, 2005.

Bartoletti, Susan Campbell. *The Journal of Finn Reardon: A Newsie*. New York: Scholastic, 2003.

Bartoletti, Susan Campbell. *Kids on Strike!* Boston: Houghton Mifflin, 1999.

Bartoletti, Susan Campbell. *No Man's Land: A Young Soldier's Story*. New York: Blue Sky, 1999.

Bartoletti, Susan Campbell. *They Called Themselves the K.K.K.: The Birth of an American Terrorist Group*. Boston: Houghton Mifflin Harcourt, 2010.

Bartoletti, Susan Campbell, and Annika Nelson. *Dancing with Dziadziu*. San Diego: Harcourt Brace, 1997.

Bartoletti, Susan Campbell, and Beppe Giacobbe. *Nobody's Diggier Than a Dog*. New York: Hyperion for Children, 2005.

Bartoletti, Susan Campbell, and Beppe Giacobbe. *Nobody's Nosier than a Cat*. New York: Hyperion for Children, 2003.

Bartoletti, Susan Campbell, and Claire A. Nivola. *The Flag Maker*. Boston: Houghton Mifflin, 2004.

Bartoletti, Susan Campbell, and David Christiana. *The Christmas Promise*. New York: Blue Sky, 2001.

Bartoletti, Susan Campbell, and David Ray. *Silver at Night*. New York: Crown, 1994.

Bartoletti, Susan Campbell, and Holly Meade. *Naamah and the Ark at Night*. Somerville, MA: Candlewick, 2011.

Michael Buckley

Buckley, Michael, and Ethen Beavers. *NERDS 2!: M Is for Mama's Boy*. New York: Amulet, 2010.

Buckley, Michael, and Ethen Beavers. *NERDS: National Espionage, Rescue, and Defense Society*. New York: Amulet, 2009.

Buckley, Michael, and Ethen Beavers. *NERDS: The Cheerleaders of Doom*. New York: Amulet, 2011.

Buckley, Michael, and Peter Ferguson. *The Council of Mirrors*. New York: Amulet, 2012.

Buckley, Michael, and Peter Ferguson. *The Everafter War*. New York: Amulet, 2009.

Buckley, Michael, and Peter Ferguson. *The Inside Story*. New York: Amulet, 2010.

Buckley, Michael, and Peter Ferguson. *Magic and Other Misdemeanors*. New York: Amulet, 2007.

Buckley, Michael, and Peter Ferguson. *Once upon a Crime*. New York: Amulet, 2007.

Buckley, Michael, and Peter Ferguson. *The Problem Child*. New York: Amulet, 2006.

Buckley, Michael, and Peter Ferguson. *The Sisters Grimm, Book One: The Fairy-Tale Detectives*. New York: Amulet, 2005.

Buckley, Michael, and Peter Ferguson. *The Sisters Grimm: The Unusual Suspects*. New York: Amulet, 2005.

Buckley, Michael, and Peter Ferguson. *The Sisters Grimm: A Very Grimm Guide*. Harry N. Abrams, 2012.

Buckley, Michael, and Peter Ferguson. *Tales from the Hood*. New York: Amulet, 2008.

Jack Gantos

Gantos, Jack. *Dead End in Norvelt*. New York: Farrar, Straus & Giroux, 2011. Newbery Award winner.

Gantos, Jack. *Desire Lines*. New York: Farrar, Straus & Giroux, 1997.

Gantos, Jack. *Heads or Tails: Stories from the Sixth Grade*. New York: Farrar, Straus & Giroux, 1994.

Gantos, Jack. *Hole in My Life*. New York: Farrar, Straus & Giroux, 2002. Printz Honor book, Robert F. Sibert Award winner.

Gantos, Jack. *I Am Not Joey Pigza*. New York: Farrar, Straus & Giroux, 2007.

Gantos, Jack. *Jack Adrift: Fourth Grade Without a Clue*. New York: Farrar, Straus & Giroux, 2003.

Gantos, Jack. *Jack on the Tracks: Four Seasons of Fifth Grade*. New York: Farrar, Straus & Giroux, 1999.

Gantos, Jack. *Jack's Black Book*. New York: Farrar, Straus & Giroux, 1997.

Gantos, Jack. *Joey Pigza Loses Control*. New York: Farrar, Straus & Giroux, 2000. Newbery Honor winner.

Gantos, Jack. *Joey Pigza Swallowed the Key*. New York: Farrar, Straus & Giroux, 1998. National Book Award finalist.

Gantos, Jack. *The Love Curse of the Rumbaughs*. New York: Farrar, Straus & Giroux, 2006.

Gantos, Jack. *What Would Joey Pigza Do?* New York: Square Fish/Farrar, Straus & Giroux, 2011.

Gantos, Jack. *Zip Six: A Novel*. Bridgehampton, NY: Bridge Works, 1996.

Gantos, Jack, and Nicole Rubel. *Back to School for Rotten Ralph*. New York: HarperCollins, 1998.

Gantos, Jack, and Nicole Rubel. *Best in Show for Rotten Ralph*. New York: Farrar, Straus & Giroux, 2005.

Gantos, Jack, and Nicole Rubel. *The Christmas Spirit Strikes Rotten Ralph*. New York: HarperFestival, 1998.

Gantos, Jack, and Nicole Rubel. *Happy Birthday Rotten Ralph*. Boston: Houghton Mifflin, 1990.

Gantos, Jack, and Nicole Rubel. *The Nine Lives of Rotten Ralph*. Boston: Houghton Mifflin for Children, 2009.

Gantos, Jack, and Nicole Rubel. *Not So Rotten Ralph*. Boston: Houghton Mifflin, 1994.

Gantos, Jack, and Nicole Rubel. *Practice Makes Perfect for Rotten Ralph*. New York: Farrar, Straus & Giroux, 2002.

Gantos, Jack, and Nicole Rubel. *Rotten Ralph*. Boston: Houghton Mifflin, 1976.

Gantos, Jack, and Nicole Rubel. *Rotten Ralph Feels Rotten*. New York: Farrar, Straus & Giroux, 2004.

Gantos, Jack, and Nicole Rubel. *Rotten Ralph Helps Out*. New York: Farrar, Straus & Giroux, 2001.

Gantos, Jack, and Nicole Rubel. *Rotten Ralph's Halloween Howl*. New York: HarperFestival, 1998.

Gantos, Jack, and Nicole Rubel. *Rotten Ralph's Rotten Christmas*. Boston: Houghton Mifflin, 1984.

Gantos, Jack, and Nicole Rubel. *Rotten Ralph's Rotten Romance*. Boston: Houghton Mifflin, 1997.

Gantos, Jack, and Nicole Rubel. *Rotten Ralph's Show and Tell*. Boston: Houghton Mifflin, 1989.

Gantos, Jack, and Nicole Rubel. *Rotten Ralph's Thanksgiving Wish*. New York: HarperFestival, 1999.

Gantos, Jack, and Nicole Rubel. *Three Strikes for Rotten Ralph*. New York: Farrar, Straus & Giroux, 2011.

Gantos, Jack, and Nicole Rubel. *Wedding Bells for Rotten Ralph*. New York: HarperCollins, 1999.

Gantos, Jack, and Nicole Rubel. *Worse Than Rotten, Ralph*. Boston: Houghton Mifflin, 1978.

Scieszka, Jon, Jack Gantos, Adam Rex, and Kate DiCamillo. *Guys Read: Funny Business*. New York: HarperCollins, 2010.

Jeff Kinney

Kinney, Jeff. *Diary of a Wimpy Kid: Cabin Fever*. New York: Amulet Books, 2011.

Kinney, Jeff. *Diary of a Wimpy Kid: Dog Days*. New York: Amulet Books, 2009.

Kinney, Jeff. *Diary of a Wimpy Kid: Greg Heffley's Journal*. New York: Amulet Books, 2007.

Kinney, Jeff. *Diary of a Wimpy Kid: Rodrick Rules*. New York: Amulet Books, 2008.

Kinney, Jeff. *Diary of a Wimpy Kid: The Last Straw*. New York: Amulet Books, 2009.

Kinney, Jeff. *Diary of a Wimpy Kid: The Ugly Truth*. New York: Amulet Books, 2010.

Kinney, Jeff. *The Wimpy Kid Do-It Yourself Book*. New York: Amulet Books, 2011.

Scieszka, Jon, and Jeff Kinney. *Guys Read: Funny Business*. New York: Walden Pond Press, 2010.

Gordon Korman

Korman, Gordon. *The Abduction*. New York: Scholastic, 2006.

Korman, Gordon. *Born to Rock*. New York: Hyperion, 2006.

Korman, Gordon. *Chasing the Falconers*. New York: Scholastic, 2005.

Korman, Gordon. *The Chicken Doesn't Skate*. New York: Scholastic, 1996.

Korman, Gordon. *The Climb*. New York: Scholastic, 2002.

Korman, Gordon. *Collision Course*. New York: Scholastic, 2011.

Korman, Gordon. *The Contest*. New York: Scholastic, 2002.

Korman, Gordon. *The Danger*. New York: Scholastic, 2003.

Korman, Gordon. *The Deep*. New York: Scholastic, 2003.

Korman, Gordon. *The Discovery*. New York: Scholastic, 2003.

Korman, Gordon. *The Emperor's Code*. New York: Scholastic, 2010.

Korman, Gordon. *Escape*. New York: Scholastic, 2001.

Korman, Gordon. *Framed*. New York: Scholastic, 2010.

Korman, Gordon. *The Fugitive Factor*. New York: Scholastic, 2005.

Korman, Gordon. *Hunting the Hunter*. New York: Scholastic, 2006.

Korman, Gordon. *Jake, Reinvented*. New York: Hyperion, 2003.

Korman, Gordon. *The Juvie Three*. New York: Hyperion, 2008.

Korman, Gordon. *Maxx Comedy: The Funniest Kid in America*. New York: Hyperion Books for Children, 2003.

Korman, Gordon. *The Medusa Plot*. New York: Scholastic, 2011.

Korman, Gordon. *No More Dead Dogs*. New York: Hyperion Books for Children, 2000.

Korman, Gordon. *Now You See Them, Now You Don't*. New York: Scholastic, 2005.

Korman, Gordon. *One False Note*. London: Scholastic, 2008.

Korman, Gordon. *Pop*. New York: Balzer & Bray, 2009.

Korman, Gordon. *Public Enemies*. New York: Scholastic, 2005.

Korman, Gordon. *Radio Fifth Grade*. New York: Scholastic, 1989.

Korman, Gordon. *The Rescue*. New York: Scholastic, 2006.

Korman, Gordon. *Schooled*. New York: Hyperion Books for Children, 2007.

Korman, Gordon. *The Search*. New York: Scholastic, 2006.

Korman, Gordon. *Shipwreck*. New York: Scholastic, 2001.

Korman, Gordon. *Showoff*. New York: Scholastic, 2012.

Korman, Gordon. *The 6th Grade Nickname Game*. New York: Hyperion Books for Children, 1998.

Korman, Gordon. *Son of the Mob*. New York: Hyperion Books for Children, 2002.

Korman, Gordon. *Son of the Mob: Hollywood Hustle*. New York: Hyperion, 2004.

Korman, Gordon. *S.O.S.* New York: Scholastic, 2011.

Korman, Gordon. *The Stowaway Solution*. New York: Scholastic, 2005.

Korman, Gordon. *The Summit*. New York: Scholastic, 2002.

Korman, Gordon. *Survival*. New York: Scholastic, 2001.

Korman, Gordon. *Swindle*. New York: Scholastic, 2008.

Korman, Gordon. *The Toilet Paper Tigers*. New York: Scholastic, 1993.

Korman, Gordon. *The Twinkie Squad*. New York: Scholastic, 1992.

Korman, Gordon. *The Ultimate Nose Picker Collection*. New York: Hyperion Books for Children, 2006.

Korman, Gordon. *The Zucchini Warriors*. New York: Scholastic, 1988.

Korman, Gordon. *This Can't Be Happening at Macdonald Hall!* New York: Scholastic, 1978.

Korman, Gordon. *Why Did the Underwear Cross the Road?* New York: Scholastic, 1994.

Korman, Gordon. *Zoobreak*. New York: Scholastic, 2009.

Korman, Gordon, and JoAnn Adinolfi. *Liar, Liar, Pants on Fire*. New York: Scholastic, 1997.

Riordan, Rick, Peter Lerangis, Gordon Korman, and Jude Watson. *Vespers Rising: The 39 Clues*. New York: Scholastic, 2011.

Jon Scieszka

Scieszka, Jon. *Garage Tales*. New York: Simon & Schuster Books for Young Readers, 2010.

Scieszka, Jon. *Guys Write for Guys Read*. New York: Viking, 2005.

Scieszka, Jon. *Knucklehead: Tall Tales & Mostly True Stories About Growing up Scieszka*. New York: Viking, 2008.

Scieszka, Jon. *Melvin Might?* New York: Simon & Schuster Books for Young Readers, 2008.

Scieszka, Jon. *Smash! Crash!* New York: Simon & Schuster Books for Young Readers, 2008.

Scieszka, Jon. *Truckery Rhymes*. New York: Simon & Schuster Books for Young Readers, 2009.

Scieszka, Jon. *Welcome to Trucktown!* New York: Simon & Schuster Books for Young Readers, 2010.

Scieszka, Jon, and Adam McCauley. *Da Wild, Da Crazy, Da Vinci*. New York: Viking, 2004.

Scieszka, Jon, and Adam McCauley. *Hey Kid, Want to Buy a Bridge?* New York: Viking, 2002.

Scieszka, Jon, and Adam McCauley. *Marco? Polo!* New York: Viking, 2006.

Scieszka, Jon, and Adam McCauley. *Me Oh Maya!* New York: Viking, 2003.

Scieszka, Jon, and Adam McCauley. *Oh Say, I Can't See*. New York: Viking, 2005.

Scieszka, Jon, and Adam McCauley. *Sam Samurai*. New York: Viking, 2001.

Scieszka, Jon, and Adam McCauley. *See You Later, Gladiator*. New York: Viking, 2000.

Scieszka, Jon, and Adam McCauley. *Viking It & Liking It*. New York: Viking/Penguin Putnam Books for Young Readers, 2002.

Scieszka, Jon, and Adam Rex. *Guys Read: Funny Business*. New York: Walden Pond Press, 2010.

Scieszka, Jon, and Daniel Adel. *The Book That Jack Wrote*. New York: Viking, 1994.

Scieszka, Jon, and David Shannon. *Robot Zot!* New York: Simon & Schuster Books for Young Readers, 2009.

Scieszka, Jon, and Lane Smith. *2095*. New York: Viking, 1995.

Scieszka, Jon, and Lane Smith. *Baloney, Henry P.* New York: Viking, 2001.

Scieszka, Jon, and Lane Smith. *Cowboy & Octopus*. New York: Viking, 2007.

Scieszka, Jon, and Lane Smith. *It's All Greek to Me*. New York: Viking, 1999.

Scieszka, Jon, and Lane Smith. *Knights of the Kitchen Table*. New York: Viking, 1991.

Scieszka, Jon, and Lane Smith. *Math Curse*. New York: Viking, 1995.

Scieszka, Jon, and Lane Smith. *The Not-So-Jolly-Roger*. New York: Viking, 1991.

Scieszka, Jon, and Lane Smith. *Science Verse*. New York: Viking, 2004.

Scieszka, Jon, and Lane Smith. *Seen Art?* New York: Viking, 2005.

Scieszka, Jon, and Lane Smith. *The Stinky Cheese Man*. New York: Penguin Books, 1992. Caldecott Honor book.

Scieszka, Jon, and Lane Smith. *Summer Reading Is Killing Me!* New York: Viking, 1998.

Scieszka, Jon, and Lane Smith. *The True Story of the 3 Little Pigs!* New York: Viking Kestrel, 1989.

Scieszka, Jon, and Lane Smith. *Tut, Tut*. New York: Viking, 1996.

Scieszka, Jon, and Lane Smith. *Your Mother Was a Neanderthal*. New York: Viking, 1993.

Scieszka, Jon, and Steve Johnson. *The Frog Prince, Continued*. New York: Viking, 1991.

Scieszka, Jon, Lane Smith, and Molly Leach. *Squids Will Be Squids: Fresh Morals, Beastly Fables*. New York: Viking, 1998.

Scieszka, Jon, M. T. Anderson, and Brett Helquist. *Guys Read: / Thriller*. New York: Walden Pond Press, 2011.

Scieszka, Jon, Mary Blair, and Lewis Carroll. *Walt Disney's Alice in Wonderland*. New York: Disney Press, 2008.

Scieszka, Jon, David Shannon, Loren Long, and David Gordon. *Dizzy Izzy*. New York: Aladdin, 2010.

Scieszka, Jon, Shane Prigmore, and Francesco Sedita. *Spaceheadz*. New York: Simon & Schuster Books for Young Readers, 2010.

Scieszka, Jon, Shane Prigmore, Casey Scieszka, and Steven Weinberg. *Spaceheadz*. New York: Simon & Schuster Books for Young Readers, 2010.

Scieszka, Jon, Shane Prigmore, Casey Scieszka, and Steven Weinberg. *Spaceheadz*. New York: Simon & Schuster Books for Young Readers, 2011.

Scieszka, Jon, David Gordon, Loren Long, and David Shannon. *Pete's Party*. New York: Aladdin, 2008.

Scieszka, Jon, David Gordon, Loren Long, and David Shannon. *Zoom! Boom! Bully*. New York: Aladdin, 2008.

Paul Volponi

Volponi, Paul. *Black and White*. New York: Viking, 2005.

Volponi, Paul. *Crossing Lines*. New York: Viking, 2011.

Volponi, Paul. *Homestretch*. New York: Atheneum for Young Readers, 2009.

Volponi, Paul. *Hurricane Song*. New York: Viking, 2008.

Volponi, Paul. *Response*. New York: Viking, 2009.

Volponi, Paul. *Rikers High*. New York: Viking, 2010.

Volponi, Paul. *Rooftop*. New York: Viking, 2006.

Volponi, Paul. *Rucker Park Setup*. New York: Viking, 2007.

Volponi, Paul. *The Final Four*. New York: Viking, 2012.

Volponi, Paul. *The Hand You're Dealt*. New York: Atheneum for Young Readers, 2008.

Jacqueline Woodson

Woodson, Jacqueline. *After Tupac & D Foster.* New York: G. P. Putnam's Sons, 2008. Newbery Honor medal.

Woodson, Jacqueline. *Behind You.* New York: G. P. Putnam's Sons, 2004. Sequel to *If You Come Softly.*

Woodson, Jacqueline. *Beneath a Meth Moon.* New York: Nancy Paulsen, 2012.

Woodson, Jacqueline. *Between Madison & Palmetto.* New York: Bantam Doubleday Dell for Young Readers, 1995. Sequel to *Maizon at Blue Hill.*

Woodson, Jacqueline. *The Dear One.* New York: Delacorte, 1991.

Woodson, Jacqueline. *Feathers.* New York: G. P. Putnam's Sons, 2007. Newbery Honor medal.

Woodson, Jacqueline. *From the Notebooks of Melanin Sun.* New York: Blue Sky, 1995. Coretta Scott King Honor book.

Woodson, Jacqueline. *The House You Pass on the Way.* New York: Delacorte, 1997.

Woodson, Jacqueline. *Hush.* New York: Putnam's, 2002. National Book Award finalist.

Woodson, Jacqueline. *I Hadn't Meant to Tell You This.* New York: Delacorte, 1994. Coretta Scott King Honor book.

Woodson, Jacqueline. *If You Come Softly.* New York: Putnam's, 1998.

Woodson, Jacqueline. *Last Summer with Maizon.* New York: Delacorte, 1990.

Woodson, Jacqueline. *Lena.* New York: Delacorte, 1999. Sequel to *I Hadn't Meant to Tell You This.*

Woodson, Jacqueline. *Locomotion.* New York: G. P. Putnam's Sons, 2003. National Book Award finalist.

Woodson, Jacqueline. *Maizon at Blue Hill.* New York: Putnam, 2002. Sequel to *Last Summer with Maizon.*

Woodson, Jacqueline. *Miracle's Boys.* New York: G. P. Putnam's Sons, 2000. Coretta Scott King Award.

Woodson, Jacqueline. *Peace, Locomotion.* New York: G. P. Putnam's Sons, 2009. Sequel to *Locomotion.*

Woodson, Jacqueline, and Diane Greenseid. *We Had a Picnic This Sunday Past.* New York: Hyperion for Children, 1997.

Woodson, Jacqueline, and Earl B. Lewis. *Coming on Home Soon.* New York: G. P. Putnam's Sons, 2004. Caldecott Honor.

Woodson, Jacqueline, and Earl B. Lewis. *The Other Side.* New York: Putnam's, 2001.

Woodson, Jacqueline, and Floyd Cooper. *Sweet, Sweet Memory*. New York: Jump at the Sun/Hyperion for Children, 2000.

Woodson, Jacqueline, and Hudson Talbott. *Show Way*. New York: G. P. Putnam's Sons, 2005. Newbery Honor medal.

Woodson, Jacqueline, and James Ransome. *Visiting Day*. New York: Scholastic, 2002.

Woodson, Jacqueline, and Jon J. Muth. *Our Gracie Aunt*. New York: Hyperion for Children/Jump at the Sun, 2002.

Woodson, Jacqueline, and Sophie Blackall. *Pecan Pie Baby*. New York: G. P. Putnam's Sons, 2010.

Children's Books Cited

Alexie, Sherman, and Ellen Forney. 2007. *The Absolutely True Diary of a Part-Time Indian*. New York: Little, Brown.

Allard, Harry, and James Marshall. 1977. *Miss Nelson Is Missing!* Boston: Houghton Mifflin.

Allen, Thomas B., and Roger MacBride Allen. 2009. *Mr. Lincoln's High-Tech War: How the North Used the Telegraph, Railroads, Surveillance Balloons, Ironclads, High-Powered Weapons, and More to Win the Civil War*. Washington, DC: National Geographic.

Anderson, Laurie Halse. 1999. *Speak*. New York: Farrar, Straus & Giroux.

Anderson, Laurie Halse. 2009. *Wintergirls*. New York: Viking.

Anderson, M. T. 2002. *Feed*. Cambridge, MA: Candlewick Press.

Angleberger, Tom. 2011. *Darth Paper Strikes Back: An Origami Yoda Book*. New York: Amulet Books.

Angleberger, Tom, and Jason L. Rosenstock. 2010. *The Strange Case of Origami Yoda*. New York: Amulet Books.

Asher, Jay. 2007. *Thirteen Reasons Why*. New York: Razorbill.

Asher, Jay, and Carolyn Mackler. 2011. *The Future of Us*. New York: Razorbill.

Avasthi, Swati. 2010. *Split*. New York: Alfred A. Knopf.

Avi. 1986. *Wolf Rider: A Tale of Terror*. New York: Bradbury Press.

Avi. 1988. *Something Upstairs: A Tale of Ghosts*. New York: Orchard Books.

Avi. 1990. *The True Confessions of Charlotte Doyle*. New York: Orchard Books.

Avi. 1991. *Windcatcher*. New York: Bradbury Press.

Babbitt, Natalie. 1975. *Tuck Everlasting*. New York: Farrar, Straus & Giroux.

Baglio, Ben M., and Jenny Gregory. 2002. *Dog at the Door*. New York: Scholastic.

Bartoletti, Susan Campbell. 2005. *Hitler Youth: Growing Up in Hitler's Shadow*. New York: Scholastic Nonfiction.

Bartoletti, Susan Campbell. 2010. *They Called Themselves the K.K.K.: The Birth of an American Terrorist Group*. Boston: Houghton Mifflin Harcourt.

Barton, Chris, and Paul Hoppe. 2011. *Can I See Your I.D.? True Stories of False Identities*. New York: Dial Books for Young Readers.

Bingham, Kelly L. 2007. *Shark Girl*. Cambridge, MA: Candlewick Press.

Bloor, Edward. 1997. *Tangerine*. San Diego: Harcourt Brace.

Blume, Judy. 1978. *Freckle Juice*. New York: Yearling Books.

Blume, Judy. 2007. *Tales of a Fourth Grade Nothing*. London: Puffin.

Blumenthal, Karen. 2011. *Bootleg: Murder, Moonshine, and the Lawless Years of Prohibition*. New York: Roaring Brook Press.

Borden, Louise. 2012. *His Name Was Raoul Wallenberg: Courage, Rescue, and Mystery During World War II*. Boston: Houghton Mifflin.

Bragg, Georgia, and Kevin O'Malley. 2011. *How They Croaked: The Awful Ends of the Awfully Famous*. New York: Walker & Co.

Brenner, Martha, and Donald Cook. 1994. *Abe Lincoln's Hat*. New York: Random House.

Brewer, Heather. 2007. *Eighth Grade Bites*. New York: Dutton Children's Books.

Brown, Don. 2011. *America Is Under Attack: September 11, 2001: The Day the Towers Fell*. New York: Roaring Brook Press.

Brown, Margaret Wise, and Clement Hurd. 1947. *Goodnight Moon*. New York: Harper & Brothers.

Buckley, Michael, and Ethen Beavers. 2009. *NERDS: National Espionage, Rescue, and Defense Society*. New York: Amulet Books.

Bunting, Eve, and David Diaz. 1994. *Smoky Night*. San Diego: Harcourt Brace.

Bunting, Eve, and Stephen Gammell. 1980. *Terrible Things*. New York: Harper & Row.

Burnett, Frances Hodgson, and Tasha Tudor. 1962. *The Secret Garden*. Philadelphia: Lippincott.

Chaltas, Thalia. 2009. *Because I Am Furniture*. New York: Viking.

Christopher, Lucy. 2010. *Stolen*. New York: Chicken House/Scholastic.

Christopher, Lucy. 2011. *Flyaway*. New York: Chicken House.

Christopher, Matt. 1986. *Dirt Bike Racer*. New York: Little, Brown.

Clark, Ann Nolan. 1952. *Secret of the Andes*. London: Puffin.

Cleary, Beverly. 1965. *The Mouse and the Motorcycle*. New York: Harper Trophy.

Clearly, Beverly. 2009. The Ramona Collection. New York: Harper Collins.

Collins, Suzanne. 2008. *The Hunger Games*. New York: Scholastic.

Collins, Suzanne. 2009. *Catching Fire*. New York: Scholastic.

Collins, Suzanne. 2010. *Mockingjay*. New York: Scholastic.

Cooper, Susan, and Alan E. Cober. 1973. *The Dark Is Rising*. New York: Atheneum.

Cummings, Priscilla. 2004. *Red Kayak*. New York: Dutton Children's Books.

Curtis, Christopher Paul. 1995. *The Watsons Go to Birmingham—1963*. New York: Yearling Books.

Curtis, Christopher Paul. 1999. *Bud, Not Buddy*. New York: Delacorte Press.

Deem, James M. 2003. *Bodies from the Bog*. Boston: Houghton Mifflin.

Deem, James M. 2005. *Bodies from the Ash: Life and Death in Ancient Pompeii*. New York: Scholastic.

Deem, James M. 2008. *Bodies from the Ice: Melting Glaciers and the Recovery of the Past*. Boston: Houghton Mifflin.

Denenberg, Barry. 2008. *Lincoln Shot: A President's Life Remembered*. New York: Feiwel & Friends.

Donnelly, Jennifer. 2003. *A Northern Light*. San Diego: Harcourt.

DuPrau, Jeanne. 2003. *The City of Ember*. New York: Random House.

Erskine, Kathryn. 2011. *Mockingbird*. New York: Puffin.

Farmer, Nancy. 2002. *The House of the Scorpion*. New York: Atheneum Books for Young Readers.

Fisher, Catherine. 2010. *Incarceron*. New York: Dial Books.

Fleischman, John. 2002. *Phineas Gage: A Gruesome but True Story About Brain Science*. Boston: Houghton Mifflin.

Fleming, Candace. 2011. *Amelia Lost: The Life and Disappearance of Amelia Earhart*. New York: Schwartz & Wade Books.

Forman, Gayle. 2009. *If I Stay: A Novel*. New York: Dutton Books.

Freedman, Russell. 1987. *Lincoln: A Photobiography*. New York: Clarion Books.

Frost, Helen. 2003. *Keesha's House*. New York: Frances Foster Books/Farrar, Straus & Giroux.

Frost, Helen. 2011. *Hidden*. New York: Farrar, Straus & Giroux.

Gaiman, Neil, and P. Craig Russell. 2002. *Coraline: Graphic Novel*. London: Bloomsbury.

Gantos, Jack. 2011. *Dead End in Norvelt*. New York: Farrar, Straus & Giroux.

Getz, David. 1994. *Frozen Man*. New York: Henry Holt.

Getz, David, and Peter McCarty. 2000. *Purple Death: The Mysterious Flu of 1918*. New York: Henry Holt.

Giovanni, Nikki, and Bryan Collier. 2008. *Lincoln and Douglass: An American Friendship*. New York: Henry Holt.

Glenn, Mel. 1996. *Who Killed Mr. Chippendale? A Mystery in Poems*. New York: Lodestar Books.

Golenbock, Peter, and Paul Bacon. 1990. *Teammates*. San Diego: Harcourt Brace Jovanovich.

Grant, Michael. 2008. *Gone*. New York: HarperTeen.

Greenfield, Eloise, and Jan Spivey Gilchrist. 1988. *Nathaniel Talking*. New York: Black Butterfly Children's Books.

Greenwald, Tom. 2011. *Charlie Joe Jackson's Guide to Not Reading*. New York: Roaring Brook Press.

Greenwald, Tom, and J. P. Coovert. 2012. *Charlie Joe Jackson's Guide to Extra Credit*. New York: Roaring Brook Press.

Hale, Shannon, Dean Hale, and Nathan Hale. 2008. *Rapunzel's Revenge*. New York: Bloomsbury.

Hatke, Ben. 2010. *Zita the Spacegirl*. New York: First Second.

Hatkoff, Isabella, Craig Hatkoff, P. Kahumbu, and Peter Greste. 2006. *Owen & Mzee: The True Story of a Remarkable Friendship*. New York: Scholastic.

Hautman, Pete. 2006. *Rash*. New York: Simon & Schuster Books for Young Readers.

Hinton, S. E. 1967. *The Outsiders*. New York: Viking Press.

Holm, Jennifer L. 2007. *Middle School Is Worse Than Meatloaf*. New York: Simon & Schuster.

Hoose, Phillip M. 2009. *Claudette Colvin: Twice Toward Justice*. New York: Melanie Kroupa Books/Farrar, Straus & Giroux.

Hopkinson, Deborah, and Brian Floca. 2005. *Billy and the Rebel: Based on a True Civil War Story*. New York: Atheneum Books for Young Readers.

Hopkinson, Deborah, and John Hendrix. 2008. *Abe Lincoln Crosses a Creek: A Tall, Thin Tale (Introducing His Forgotten Frontier Friend)*. New York: Schwartz & Wade Books.

Horowitz, Anthony. 2001. *Stormbreaker*. New York: Philomel.

Horowitz, Anthony, Antony Johnston, Kanako Damerum, and Yuzuru Takasaki. 2007. *Point Blank: The Graphic Novel*. New York: Philomel Books.

Horowitz, Anthony, Antony Johnston, Kanako Damerum, and Yuzuru Takasaki. 2009. *Skeleton Key Graphic Novel*. London: Walker.

Horowitz, Anthony, Antony Johnston, Kanako Damerum, Yuzuru Takasaki, and Anthony Horowitz. 2006. *Stormbreaker: The Graphic Novel*. New York: Philomel.

Ignatow, Amy. 2010. *The Popularity Papers: Research for the Social Improvement and General Betterment of Lydia Goldblatt & Julie Graham-Chang*. New York: Amulet Books.

Innocenti, Roberto, Christophe Gallaz, Martha Coventry, Richard Graglia, and G. M. Tschudi. 1985. *Rose Blanche*. Mankato, MN: Creative Education.

Katz, Jon. 2011. *Meet the Dogs of Bedlam Farm*. New York: Henry Holt.

Kinney, Jeff. 2007. *Diary of a Wimpy Kid: Greg Heffley's Journal*. New York: Amulet Books.

Koertge, Ronald. 2003. *Shakespeare Bats Cleanup*. Cambridge, MA: Candlewick Press.

Korman, Gordon. 2009. *Pop*. New York: Balzer & Bray.

Krensky, Stephen, and Gershom Griffith. 2002. *Abe Lincoln and the Muddy Pig*. New York: Aladdin.

Krosoczka, Jarrett. 2009. *Lunch Lady*. New York: Alfred A. Knopf.

Krull, Kathleen, and David Diaz. 1996. *Wilma Unlimited: How Wilma Rudolph Became the World's Fastest Woman*. San Diego: Harcourt Brace.

LaFleur, Suzanne. 2009. *Love, Aubrey*. New York: Random House/Yearling.

Larson, Kirby, Mary Nethery, and Jean Cassels. 2008. *Two Bobbies: A True Story of Hurricane Katrina, Friendship, and Survival*. New York: Walker.

Law, Ingrid. 2010. *Savvy*. New York: Dial Books for Young Readers.

Lee, Harper. 1960. *To Kill a Mockingbird*. Philadelphia, PA: J. B. Lippincott.

Lincoln, Abraham, and Michael McCurdy. 1998. *The Gettysburg Address*. Boston: Houghton Mifflin.

Lord, Cynthia. 2010. *Touch Blue*. New York: Scholastic.

Lowry, Lois. 1993. *The Giver*. Boston: Houghton Mifflin.

Magoon, Kekla. 2011. *Camo Girl*. New York: Aladdin.

Malone, Marianne, and Greg Call. 2010. *The Sixty-Eight Rooms*. New York: Random House.

Marrin, Albert. 2002. *Dr. Jenner and the Speckled Monster: The Search for the Smallpox Vaccine*. New York: Dutton Children's Books.

Marrin, Albert. 2011. *Flesh and Blood So Cheap: The Triangle Fire and Its Legacy*. New York: Alfred A. Knopf.

McCloud, Scott. 2006. *Making Comics: Storytelling Secrets of Comics, Manga and Graphic Novels*. New York: William Morrow.

McCormick, Patricia. 2006. *Sold*. New York: Hyperion.

McDonnell, Patrick. 2011. *Me . . . Jane*. New York: Little, Brown.

Meyer, Stephenie. 2005. *Twilight.* New York: Little, Brown.

Meyer, Stephenie. 2006. *New Moon.* New York: Little, Brown.

Meyer, Stephenie. 2007. *Eclipse.* New York: Little, Brown.

Meyer, Stephenie. 2008. *Breaking Dawn.* New York: Little, Brown.

Mochizuki, Ken, and Dom Lee. 1997. *Passage to Freedom: The Sugihara Story.* New York: Lee & Low.

Montgomery, Sy. 2012. *Temple Grandin: How the Girl Who Loved Cows Embraced Autism and Changed the World.* Boston: Houghton Mifflin Books for Children/Houghton Mifflin Harcourt.

Murphy, Jim. 2003. *An American Plague: The True and Terrifying Story of the Yellow Fever Epidemic of 1793.* Boston: Clarion Books.

Murphy, Jim, and Alison Blank. 2012. *Invincible Microbe: Tuberculosis and the Never-Ending Search for a Cure.* Boston: Clarion Books.

Myers, Walter Dean, and Christopher Myers. 1999. *Monster.* New York: HarperCollins.

Naylor, Phyllis Reynolds. 1991. *Shiloh.* New York: Atheneum.

Nelson, Kadir. 2011. *Heart and Soul: The Story of America and African Americans.* New York: Balzer & Bray.

Neri, Greg, and Jesse Joshua Watson. 2007. *Chess Rumble.* New York: Lee & Low.

Neri, Greg, and Randy DuBurke. 2010. *Yummy: The Last Days of a Southside Shorty.* New York: Lee & Low.

Ness, Patrick. 2008, 2009, 2010. Chaos Walking series. Cambridge, MA: Candlewick Press.

Newquist, HP 2012. *The Book of Blood: From Legends and Leeches to Vampires and Veins.* Boston: Houghton Mifflin Books for Children.

O'Connell, Caitlin, Donna M. Jackson, and T. C. Rodwell. 2011. *The Elephant Scientist.* Boston: Houghton Mifflin Books for Children.

Park, Linda Sue. 2001. *A Single Shard.* Boston, MA: Houghton Mifflin Harcourt.

Partridge, Elizabeth, and Jim Hoover. 2009. *Marching for Freedom: Walk Together, Children, and Don't You Grow Weary.* New York: Viking.

Pascal, Janet B., and John O'Brien. 2008. *Who Was Abraham Lincoln?* New York: Grosset & Dunlap.

Patent, Dorothy Hinshaw, and William Muñoz. 2011. *Saving Audie: A Pit Bull Puppy Gets a Second Chance.* New York: Walker & Co.

Paterson, Katherine, and Donna Diamond. 1977. *Bridge to Terabithia.* New York: Crowell.

Patterson, James. 2007. *Maximum Ride: The Angel Experiment*. New York: Little, Brown.

Patterson, James, Christopher Tebbetts, and Laura Park. 2011. *Middle School, the Worst Years of My Life*. New York: Little, Brown.

Paulsen, Gary. 1996. *Hatchet*. Boston, MA: Houghton Mifflin.

Paulsen, Gary. 2007. *Lawn Boy*. New York: Wendy Lamb Books.

Peirce, Lincoln. 2010. *Big Nate: In a Class by Himself*. New York: Harper.

Pfeffer, Susan Beth. 2006. *Life As We Knew It*. Orlando, FL: Harcourt.

Pilkey, Dav. 1999. *Captain Underpants*. New York: Scholastic.

Rappaport, Doreen, and Bryan Collier. 2001. *Martin's Big Words: The Life of Dr. Martin Luther King, Jr.* New York: Hyperion Books for Children.

Rappaport, Doreen, and Kadir Nelson. 2008. *Abe's Honest Words: The Life of Abraham Lincoln*. New York: Hyperion Books for Children.

Riordan, Rick. 2010. *The Lightning Thief*. New York: Miramax Books/Hyperion Books for Children.

Rosoff, Meg. 2004. *How I Live Now*. New York: Wendy Lamb Books.

Roth, Veronica. 2011. *Divergent*. New York: Katherine Tegen Books.

Rowling, J. K., and Mary GrandPré. 1998. *Harry Potter and the Sorcerer's Stone*. New York: A. A. Levine Books.

Russell, Rachel Renée. 2009. *Dork Diaries: Tales from a Not-So-Fabulous Life*. New York: Aladdin.

Ryan, Carrie. 2010. *The Forest of Hands and Teeth*. New York: Random House.

Sandler, Martin W. 2008. *Lincoln Through the Lens: How Photography Revealed and Shaped an Extraordinary Life*. New York: Walker.

Schanzer, Rosalyn. 2011. *Witches! The Absolutely True Tale of Disaster in Salem*. Washington, DC: National Geographic.

Schroeder, Lisa. 2008. *I Heart You, You Haunt Me*. New York: Simon Pulse.

Schroeder, Lisa. 2009. *Far from You*. New York: Simon Pulse.

Schroeder, Lisa. 2010. *Chasing Brooklyn*. New York: Simon Pulse.

Scieszka, Jon. 2008. *Knucklehead: Tall Tales & Mostly True Stories About Growing Up Scieszka*. New York: Viking.

Scieszka, Jon, and Lane Smith. 1989. *The True Story of the 3 Little Pigs!* New York: Viking Kestrel.

Scieszka, Jon, and Lane Smith. 1991. *The Not-So-Jolly Roger: The Time Warp Trio*. New York: Puffin.

Scieszka, Jon, and Lane Smith. 2004. *Science Verse*. New York: Viking.

Scott, Elaine. 2012. *Buried Alive! How 33 Miners Survived 69 Days Deep Under the Chilean Desert.* Boston: Houghton Mifflin Harcourt.

Selznick, Brian. 2007. *The Invention of Hugo Cabret: A Novel in Words and Pictures.* New York: Scholastic.

Shusterman, Neal. 2007. *Unwind.* New York: Simon & Schuster Books for Young Readers.

Sisulu, Elinor, and Sharon Wilson. 1996. *The Day Gogo Went to Vote: South Africa, April 1994.* Boston: Little, Brown.

Sitomer, Alan Lawrence. 2007. *Homeboyz.* New York: Jump at the Sun/ Hyperion Books for Children.

Smith, Jeff, and Steve Hamaker. 2005. *Out from Boneville.* New York: Graphix/Scholastic.

Smith, Roland. *Peak.* 2008. Orlando, FL: Harcourt Children's Books.

Stiefvater, Maggie. 2009. *Shiver.* New York: Scholastic.

Stiefvater, Maggie. 2010. *Forever.* New York: Scholastic.

Stiefvater, Maggie. 2010. *Linger.* New York: Scholastic.

Stone, Tanya Lee. 2010. *The Good, the Bad, and the Barbie: A Doll's History and Her Impact on Us.* New York: Viking.

Swanson, James L. 2009. *Chasing Lincoln's Killer.* New York: Scholastic.

Swope, Sam, and Barry Root. 1989. *The Araboolies of Liberty Street.* New York: Potter.

Tamaki, Mariko, and Jillian Tamaki. 2008. *Skim.* Toronto: Groundwood Books.

Tarshis, Lauren. 2009. *Emma-Jean Lazarus Fell in Love.* New York: Dial Books for Young Readers.

Telgemeier, Raina. 2010. *Smile.* New York: Graphix.

Thimmesh, Catherine. 2006. *Team Moon: How 400,000 People Landed Apollo 11 on the Moon.* Boston: Houghton Mifflin.

Tsuchiya, Yukio, and Ted Lewin. 1988. *Faithful Elephants: A True Story of Animals, People, and War.* Boston: Houghton Mifflin.

Turner, Ann Warren, and Ronald Himler. 1987. *Nettie's Trip South.* New York: Macmillan.

Turner, Ann Warren, and Wendell Minor. 2001. *Abe Lincoln Remembers.* New York: HarperCollins.

Van Allsburg, Chris. 1984. *The Mysteries of Harris Burdick.* Boston: Houghton Mifflin.

Van Allsburg, Chris. 1986. *The Stranger.* Boston: Houghton Mifflin.

Van Allsburg, Chris. 1992. *The Widow's Broom*. Boston: Houghton Mifflin.

Van Allsburg, Chris. 1993. *The Sweetest Fig*. Boston: Houghton Mifflin.

Venditti, Robert, Attila Futaki, and Rick Riordan. 2010. *The Lightning Thief: The Graphic Novel*. New York: Disney/Hyperion Books.

Volponi, Paul. 2007. *Rucker Park Setup*. New York: Viking.

Walker, Sally M. 2005. *Secrets of a Civil War Submarine: Solving the Mysteries of the* H. L. Hunley. Minneapolis: Carolrhoda Books.

Walker, Sally M. 2011. *Blizzard of Glass: The Halifax Explosion of 1917*. New York: Henry Holt.

Ward, Rachel. 2010. *Num8ers*. New York: Chicken House/Scholastic.

Warner, Gertrude Chandler. 1977. *The Boxcar Children*. Chicago: Albert Whitman.

Weeks, Sarah. 2011. *Pie*. New York: Scholastic.

Wells, Rosemary, and Patrick James Lynch. 2009. *Lincoln and His Boys*. Somerville, MA: Candlewick Press.

Westerfeld, Scott. Various. Uglies series. New York: Simon Pulse.

White, E. B. 1952. *Charlotte's Web*. New York: Harper Collins.

Wild, Margaret. 2004. *Jinx*. New York: Simon Pulse.

Wilder, Laura Ingalls, and Garth Williams. 1953. *Little House on the Prairie*. New York: Harper & Bros.

Wiles, Deborah, and Jerome Lagarrigue. 2001. *Freedom Summer*. New York: Atheneum Books for Young Readers.

Williams, Stanley "Tookie," and Barbara Cottman Becnel. 1998. *Life in Prison*. New York: Morrow Junior Books.

Winter, Jeanette. 2008. *Wangari's Trees of Peace: A True Story from Africa*. Orlando, FL: Houghton Mifflin Harcourt.

Winters, Kay, and Nancy Carpenter. 2002. *Abe Lincoln: The Boy Who Loved Books*. New York: Simon & Schuster.

Woodson, Jacqueline. 2003. *Locomotion*. New York: G. P. Putnam's Sons.

Woodson, Jacqueline. 2008. *After Tupac & D Foster*. New York: G. P. Putnam's Sons.

Woodson, Jacqueline. 2009. *Peace, Locomotion*. New York: G. P. Putnam's Sons.

Zarr, Sara. 2007. *Story of a Girl: A Novel*. New York: Little, Brown.

Zusak, Markus. 2006. *The Book Thief*. New York: Alfred A. Knopf.

References

Allington, Richard L. 2002. "What I've Learned About Effective Reading Instruction from a Decade of Studying Exemplary Elementary Classroom Teachers." *Phi Delta Kappan* 83 (10): 740–47.

Allington, Richard L. 2002. "You Can't Learn Much from Books You Can't Read." *Educational Leadership* 60 (3): 16–19.

Alvermann, D. E. 2001. "Reading Adolescents' Reading Identities: Looking Back to See Ahead." *Journal of Adolescent and Adult Literacy* 44 (98): 676–90.

Alvermann, Donna E. 2002. "Effective Literacy Instruction for Adolescents." *Journal of Literacy Research* 32 (2): 189–208.

Anderman, L. H., and C. Midgley. 1997. "Motivation and Middle School Students." In *What Current Research Says to the Middle Level Practitioner*, edited by J. L. Irvin, 41–48. Columbus, OH: National Middle School Association.

Applebee, A. N., J. A. Langer, M. Nystrand, and A. Gamoran. 2003. "Discussion-based Approaches to Developing Understanding: Classroom Instruction and Student Performance in Middle and High School English." *American Educational Research Journal* 40 (3): 685–730.

Atwell, Nancie. 1987. *In the Middle*. Portsmouth, NH: Heinemann.

Beers, G. Kylene. 2003. *When Kids Can't Read, What Teachers Can Do: A Guide for Teachers, 6–12*. Portsmouth, NH: Heinemann.

Beers, G. Kylene, Robert E. Probst, and Linda Rief. 2007. *Adolescent Literacy: Turning Promise into Practice*. Portsmouth, NH: Heinemann.

Brozo, William G. 2002. *To Be a Boy, to Be a Reader: Engaging Teen and Preteen Boys in Active Literacy*. Newark, DE: International Reading Association.

Chik, P. Y. 2005. "Humor and Reading Motivation in Hong Kong Elementary School Children." Proceedings of International Conference on Imagination & Education, Simon Fraser University, Canada.

Clay, Marie. 1993. *Reading Recovery: A Guidebook for Teachers in Training*. Portsmouth, NH: Heinemann.

Davis, H. A. 2003. "Conceptualizing the Role and Influence of Student-Teacher Relationships on Children's Social and Cognitive Development." *Educational Psychologist* 38: 207–34.

Donahue, P. L., M. C. Daane, and Y. Jin. 2005. "The Nation's Report Card: Reading 2003." (Publication No. NCES 2005-453) Washington, DC: U.S. Government Printing Office.

Fisher, Douglas, and Gay Ivey. March 2007. "Farewell to *A Farewell to Arms*: Deemphasizing the Whole-Class Novel." *Phi Delta Kappan* 88 (7): 494–97.

Gallagher, Kelly, and Richard L. Allington. 2009. *Readicide: How Schools Are Killing Reading and What You Can Do About It.* Portland, ME: Stenhouse Publishers.

Gambrell, Linda B. 2011. "Seven Rules of Engagement: What's Most Important to Know About Motivation to Read." *The Reading Teacher* 65 (3): 172–78.

Grigg, W. S., M. C. Daane, Y. Jin, and J. R. Campbell. 2003. "The Nation's Report Card: Reading 2002." (Publication No. NCES 2003-521) Washington, DC: U.S. Government Printing Office.

Guthrie, John T. *Engaging Adolescents in Reading.* 2008. Thousand Oaks, CA: Corwin Press.

Guthrie, John T., Allan Wigfield, and Kathleen C. Perencevich. 2004. *Motivating Reading Comprehension: Concept-Oriented Reading Instruction.* Mahwah, NJ: L. Erlbaum Associates.

Guthrie, John T., Shafer William, Y. Yin Wang, and Peter Afflerbach. 1995. "Relationships of Instruction to Amount of Reading: An Exploration of Social, Cognitive, and Instructional Connections." *Reading Research Quarterly* 30 (1): 8.

Guthrie, J. T., W. D. Schafer, Y. Y. Yang, and P. Afflerbach. 1995. "Relationships of Instruction to Amount of Reading: An Exploration of Social, Cognitive, and Instructional Connections." *Reading Research Quarterly* 30 (1): 8–25.

Ivey, Gay. 1999. "A Multicase Study in the Middle School: Complexities Among Young Adolescent Readers." *Reading Research Quarterly* 32 (2): 172–92.

Ivey, Gay. 2010. "Texts That Matter." *Educational Leadership* 67 (6): 18–23.

Ivey, Gay. 2011. "What Not to Read: A Book Intervention." *Voices from the Middle* 19 (2): 22–26.

Ivey, Gay, and Douglas Fisher. 2006. *Creating Literacy-Rich Schools for Adolescents.* Alexandria, VA: Association for Supervision and Curriculum Development.

Ivey, Gay, and Karen Broaddus. 2001. "'Just Plain Reading': A Survey of What Makes Students Want to Read in Middle School Classrooms." *Reading Research Quarterly* 36 (4): 350–77.

Ivey, Gay, and Karen Broaddus. 2007. "A Formative Experiment Investigating Literacy Engagement Among Adolescent Latina/o Students Just Beginning to Read, Write, and Speak English." *Reading Research Quarterly* 42 (4): 512–45.

Jewett, Pamela C., Jennifer L. Wilson, and Michelle A. Vanderburg. 2011. "The Unifying Power of a Whole-school Read." *Journal of Adolescent & Adult Literacy* 54 (6): 415–25.

Johnston, Peter H., Gay Ivey, and Amy Faulkner. 2011. "Talking in Class: Remembering What Is Important about Classroom Talk." *The Reading Teacher* 65 (4): 232–37.

Knoester, Matthew. Spring 2011. "Independent Reading and the 'Social Turn'" Networks: An On-Line Journal for Teacher Research. http://journals .library.wisc.edu/index.php/networks/issue/view/38.

Kohlberg, Lawrence. 1981. *The Philosophy of Moral Development.* New York: Harper & Row.

Lee, Carol D. 2006. *Culture, Literacy, and Learning: Taking Bloom in the Midst of the Whirlwind.* New York: Teachers College Press.

Lenski, Susan Davis, and Jill Lewis. 2008. *Reading Success for Struggling Adolescent Learners.* New York: Guilford Press.

Levine, R., Rathbun, A., Selden, R., and Davis, A. 1998. "NAEP's Constituents: What Do They Want? Report of the National Assessment of Educational Progress Constituents' Survey and Focus Groups." (Publication No. NCES 98521). Washington, DC: U.S. Government Printing Office.

Liang, Lauren A. 2002. "On the Shelves of the Local Library: High-Interest, Easy Reading Trade Books for Struggling Middle School and High School Readers." *Preventing School Failure* 46 (4): 183–88.

Lowry, Lois. "The Giver: A Message from the Author." Random House. Accessed March 05, 2012. http://www.randomhouse.com/teachers/ guides/give.html.

McGhee, Paul Edward. 1979. *Humor: Its Origin and Development.* San Francisco: W. H. Freeman.

Mallette, M. H., W. A. Henk, and S. A. Melnick. 2004. "The Influence of Accelerated Reader on the Affective Literacy Orientations of Intermediate Grade Students." *Journal of Literacy Research* 36 (1): 73–84.

Miller, Donalyn. 2009. *The Book Whisperer: Awakening the Inner Reader in Every Child.* San Francisco, CA: Jossey-Bass.

Moje, Elizabeth B. 2008. "Foregrounding the Disciplines in Secondary Literacy Teaching and Learning: A Call for Change." *Journal of Adolescent & Adult Literacy* 52 (2): 96–107.

Mulhern, Sarah. "Student-Led Book Clubs." The Reading Zone. Accessed March 05, 2012. http://thereadingzone.wordpress.com/2009/06/13/ student-led-book-clubs/.

National Center for Education Statistics. 2010. *The Nation's Report Card: Reading 2009* (NCES 2010-458). Washington, DC: Institute of Education Sciences, U.S. Department of Education.

Newkirk, Thomas. 2002. *Misreading Masculinity: Boys, Literacy, and Popular Culture*. Portsmouth, NH: Heinemann.

Otis, Nancy, Frederick M. E. Grouzet, and Luc G. Pelletier. 2005. "Latent Motivational Change in an Academic Setting: A 3-Year Longitudinal Study." *Journal of Educational Psychology* 97 (2): 170–83.

Raphael, T. E. 1982. "Question-Answering Strategies for Children." *The Reading Teacher* 36 (2): 186–90.

Rasinski, Timothy. 2003. *The Fluent Reader: Oral Reading Strategies for Building Word Recognition, Fluency, and Comprehension*. New York: Scholastic.

Reeve, Johnmarshall, and Hyungshim Jang. 2006. "What Teachers Say and Do to Support Students' Autonomy During a Learning Activity." *Journal of Educational Psychology* 98 (1): 209–18.

Robb, Laura. 2000. *Teaching Reading in Middle School: A Strategic Approach to Teaching Reading That Improves Comprehension and Thinking*. New York: Scholastic.

Smith, Frank. 1998. *The Book of Learning and Forgetting*. New York: Teachers College Press.

Smith, Michael W., and Jeffrey D. Wilhelm. 2002. *Reading Don't Fix No Chevys: Literacy in the Lives of Young Men*. Portsmouth, NH: Heinemann.

Strickland, Dorothy S., and Donna E. Alvermann. 2004. *Bridging the Literacy Achievement Gap, Grades 4–12*. New York: Teachers College Press.

Trelease, Jim. 2001. *The Read-Aloud Handbook*. New York: Penguin.

Wilhelm, Jeffrey D. 1997. *"You Gotta BE the Book": Teaching Engaged and Reflective Reading with Adolescents*. New York: Teachers College Press.

Worthy, Jo, and Sharon S. McKool. 1996. "Students Who Say They Hate to Read: The Importance of Opportunity, Choice, and Access." In *Literacies for the 21st Century: Research and Practice*, edited by D. Leu, C. Kinzer, and K. Hinchman, 245–56. Chicago: National Reading Conference.